Guillemette Delaporte

René Herbst
Pioneer of Modernism

Flammarion

Translated from the French by David Radzinowicz

Editorial Direction
Suzanne Tise-Isoré

Editorial Coordination
Sandrine Balihaut Martin

Copyediting
Christine Schultz-Touge

Typesetting
Emmanuel Laparra

Color Separation
Christian Guisiano, Nuance Graphique, Paris

Distributed in North America by Rizzoli International Publications, Inc.

Simultaneously published in French as *René Herbst, pionnier du mouvement moderne*
© Éditions Flammarion, 2004
© UCAD/Bibliothèque des Arts décoratifs, 2004
English-language edition
© Éditions Flammarion, 2004
© UCAD/Bibliothèque des Arts décoratifs, 2004

www.editions.flammarion.com

04 05 06 4 3 2 1

FC0467-04-X
ISBN: 2-0803-0467-4
Dépôt légal: 10/2004

Printed in Italy

Also published in collaboration with the Bibliothèque des Arts Décoratifs:
Atget, Paris in Detail, in the collection "Photographs of the Nineteenth Century,"
Éditions Flammarion/UCAD, May 2002. Collection Director: Josiane Sartre.

Guillemette Delaporte

René Herbst
Pioneer of Modernism

Collection "Archives of Twentieth-Century Interior Architecture"
Bibliothèque des Arts Décoratifs, Paris

Flammarion  union centrale
union centrale des arts décoratifs
des arts décoratifs

In memory of my father, engineer and humanist

My gratitude must go first to Josiane Sartre, chief curator of the Bibliothèque des Arts Décoratifs, who understood the interest of publishing these archives of twentieth-century interior architecture, commencing with the Fonds René Herbst, and to Suzanne Tise-Isoré of Éditions Flammarion for shepherding the project so enthusiastically.

My heartfelt thanks go to Madame Lise Michaud-Herbst and her children who granted permission to publish the Fonds.

I would in addition like to thank Réjane Bargiel and Michèle Jasnin at the Musée de la Publicité and Rachel Brishoual at the photo library of the Musée des Arts Décoratifs for their assistance.

Sandrine Balihaut Martin and Emmanuel Laparra have also offered valuable support in preparing this book.

I would like to acknowledge the patience and kindness of my colleagues at the Bibliothèque: Béatrice Krikorian, Lysiane Alinieu, Laure Haberschill, Yann Onfroy, and Carole Balut.

Thank you, finally, to my daughter Lucile, who has had to put up with many an evening and weekend sacrificed to this endeavor.

CONTENTS

JOSIANE SARTRE PREFACE

"President Robert Bordaz has recently learned . . . that it is your intention to deposit at the Union Centrale des Arts Décoratifs photographic and bibliographical documents pertaining to your work. . . . You have represented French art. . . . In this manner, an aspect of art history in which we are personally engaged will enter the Union Centrale des Arts Décoratifs." August 18, 1982.[1]

That same August 1982, the René Herbst Archives entered the Bibliothèque des Arts Décoratifs. On September 29, in Paris, René Herbst passed away. His gift was thus the final legacy of this architect-decorator—a leading figure in the modern movement from the 1930s to the postwar period—to the Union Centrale des Arts Décoratifs. Their first encounter dated back to 1925, to the occasion of the International Exhibition of Decorative Arts organized by the Union Centrale des Arts Décoratifs. Postponed due to World War I, the germ of the exhibition had been born as early as 1911, and had rallied pioneers in modern art in France of the caliber of Rene Guilleré, founder of the Société des Artistes Décorateurs in 1901, Frantz Jourdain, the architect of La Samaritaine and founder of the Salon d'Automne in 1903, and François Carnot, president of the same Union Centrale des Arts Décoratifs. The first two luminaries had declared that "Art is one," had preached equality between fine and applied arts, and had militated for a socially committed art. Meanwhile, since 1910, the third had been piloting an association whose 1864 act of foundation stipulated its commitment "to promoting artistic culture in France and to pursuing the advent of the 'beautiful in the useful.'" René Herbst, who had already attracted attention at the 1921 Salon d'Automne with his *Coin de repos* composed of a bow-window and alcove in which the furniture was embedded, sat on the jury for exhibition admissions, as well as being secretary to the steering committee. He was also responsible for decorating five luxury stores on the Alexander III Bridge, including his own René-Herbst Décoration. There were some, however, who shared his opinion that their efforts had been insufficiently represented at this showpiece event. In 1928, the René Herbst group, with Charlotte Perriand and Djo-Bourgeois, started staging their own exhibits within the ambit of the Salon des Artistes Décorateurs. Then, in 1929, the young group split off from the Salon des Artistes Décorateurs to establish, together with Robert Mallet-Stevens, Francis Jourdain, and Gérard Sandoz, among others, the UAM—the Union des Artistes Modernes—the guiding principle of which was to promote a truly social art in opposition to the decorative and ornamental style in vogue. UAM's debut exposition took place from June 11 to July 14, 1930 at the Musée des Arts Décoratifs in the Pavillon de Marsan. René Herbst presented a Pleyel piano in mahogany and nickel-plate, a nickel-plated bridge table, four nickel-plate and rubber chairs, and a nickel-plated and mahogany sideboard. The textiles were by Hélène Henry.[2] In 1932, at the third UAM exhibition, similarly held at the Musée des Arts Décoratifs, Herbst showed a dressing table made for the Princess Aga Khan. The choice of materials—glass and metal—was roundly condemned. Dispersed during World War II, the members of the Union joined forces once again in the *Manifeste* of 1949 in which they stated their intention to forge an art for their own time, covering everything from town planning "to the humblest everyday article." Their ideas found their application in the exhibition *Formes Utiles, objets de notre temps,* once again staged at the Musée des Arts Décoratifs, in the main hall, during December 1949. The exhibition was held under the high patronage of Eugène Claudius-Petit, Minister for Reconstruction and Urbanism, the President of the UCAD being François Carnot and the President of the UAM, René Herbst himself. The prologue, by André Hermant, vice-president of the UAM, pleaded for harmony and simplicity in the home and amounted to a manifesto. The exhibition "Formes Utiles," he wrote, "intends to show that in 1950 there exist everyday objects, produced by craftsmen or industrials, accessible in price, of high quality, and in forms that add to the harmony of daily life."[3] It was a notion that echoed the motto of the UCAD, "the beautiful in the useful." "Within the walls of the Musée des Arts Décoratifs," Hermant went on, "in which the legacy of centuries past proclaims the unceasing renewal of forms—modern 'styles' of every period—this array of simple objects from our own time is meant to be understood as symbolic." Over the following twenty years, René Herbst continued to exercise his talents at the Musée des Arts Décoratifs, this time as a technical curator involved in prestigious exhibitions that broke new ground and that remain etched in the collective memory: in 1956–1957, the First Triennial of contemporary French art, *Art et*

Techniques, Formes Utiles, in which numerous members of the UAM showed their work; in 1962, *Vie Quotidienne* (Daily Life); the following year, *Formes Industrielles,* an international selection for which René Herbst sat as vice-president on the organizing committee. An account of these regular contacts between René Herbst and the Union Centrale des Arts Décoratifs is in effect a chapter in the story of modern decorative arts over a period of some fifty years, and, if René Herbst answers the definition proposed by Guillemette Delaporte, *René Herbst, Pioneer of Modern Design,* then the Union Centrale des Arts Décoratifs surely does likewise. Basing her findings on these archives, which incorporate a substantial number of photographs and published documents, Guillemette Delaporte has reconstructed every stage of René Herbst's multifaceted oeuvre and influence. Indeed, there are so many aspects to his personality that it is hard to know which one to stress: the display consultant, lighting designer, and exhibition scenographer—or the education luminary, the designer of glass and metal furniture (so innovative in its use of elastic straps for seating), the founder of the UAM,—and the dissenting voice on the manifesto of July 14, 1934, *Pour l'art moderne.* After immersing him- or herself in this thorough yet lively text, enriched with an extraordinary wealth of illustrations from the Archives now conserved at the Bibliothèque des Arts Décoratifs, the final choice will have to be the reader's.

Josiane Sartre is Chief Curator at the Bibliothèque des Arts Décoratifs.
1. Letter dated August 18, 1982 from the *délégué général* of the UCAD, Daniel Janicot, addressed to René Herbst. UCAD Archives. **2.** First exhibition of the UAM, catalog, René Herbst, p. 17.
3. Catalog of the exhibition *Formes Utiles, objets de notre temps,* presented by André Hermant, non-paginated.

AT THE BEGINNING
OF MODERNISM

1

AFTER THE GREAT WAR

"The Great War occasioned a much deeper rift than has been supposed. After a night-mare that had lasted some five years, the younger generation of interior decorators who returned to take up their tools and drawing-pens had lost contact with the art of 1908–1914. They felt the need to do something—but more especially to do something different. With the gusto of barbarians, in the École des Arts Décoratifs they wreaked havoc with its teaching. . . . They had survived in the trenches in the shadow of mighty iron: on their return, they wanted to find a place for it in houses as well, and so they transformed the aesthetics of home furnishing." HENRI CLOUZOT, 1933[1]

René Herbst's career commenced in 1908. On completing architecture studies in Paris, he went on a training course to England, where he took part as—according to his own expression—a "runner [*grouillot*]" at the Franco-British Exhibition in London, before moving to Frankfurt, Germany. At this time, both countries were cradles of the Art Nouveau movement about to sweep Europe. World War I, however, brought these travels to an abrupt halt and, for the next seven years, Herbst was mobilized in the air force, before entering the reserves.

At the onset of this first modern war, it was in the recently instituted air force that technological innovation triumphed. The role played by Cubist painters in the creation of camouflage, a necessary adjunct to the exploitation of airspace, and the war's impact on artists generally, in particular on André Mare whose war notebooks have been published[2] and exhibited,[3] is now well documented.

The war though did create a breach: nothing could ever be the same again, in the social as well as the intellectual spheres. While in 1919–1920 the architect Louis Süe was utilizing wood stockpiled for warplane manufacture to make dining rooms suites, René Herbst was about to launch out into the manufacture of metal furniture.

■ Page 5: Colonial Exhibition, Paris, 1931, "Metropolitan Section," iron and steel industries. Architecture and installation by René Herbst for OTUA.
Page 11: Self-portrait of René Herbst. Photomontage on the cover of a file.

AFTER THE GREAT WAR

A fervent advocate of the fledgling domain of the industrial arts, René Herbst was to put recent technical developments to good use: in addition to making metal furniture, he was also to design integrated lighting systems and line walls with rubber to improve sound-proofing in concrete constructions. Moreover, he ushered in a veritable revolution in store architecture, as well as in the art of shop display, founding a journal, *Parade*, to the purpose. Asked in 1936 what had spurred him to embark on this program of reform, he replied:

> "The notion arose on my return from the war. The mood of the war had been space and air; it had spirited us away from the stifling atmosphere of the city, from our daily routine. Demobilized at the Armistice, I thought of myself as a sailor thrown up on dry land, in a new country, seeing it with fresh eyes. The defects of the city where I was meant to start living once again struck me forcibly. Everything seemed backward-looking, everything seemed false."[4]

PIONEERS OF MODERNITY IN FRANCE

In France, modernity was embodied in personalities such as Frantz Jourdain, the architect of La Samaritaine department store. At the 1889 Universal Exhibition, Jourdain had written: "Today decoration reigns supreme in the interior as well as the exterior of the Universal Exhibition center . . . an alliance . . . which demonstrates that it is utopian to think of demarcating roles in the building industry, to allot, for example, the construction of the carcass to one and the responsibility of facing it, furnishing it, and endowing it with a soul to another."[5]

The battle lines between the major and minor arts were now drawn up. "Art is One," promoters of Art Nouveau declared, and, gradually, it was they who began to occupy center stage. At the Universal Exhibition of 1900, at the instigation of Frantz Jourdain who had militated for the arts to be treated equally, the Société des Artistes Français and the Société

■ Page 13: René Herbst (standing) in the company of Robert and Andrée Mallet-Stevens.
Facing page: René-Herbst Décoration store on the Alexander III Bridge, Paris. International Exhibition of Decorative Arts, 1925. Store-front, furniture, objects, and silhouette dummy by Herbst.

PIONEERS OF MODERNITY IN FRANCE

Nationale des Beaux-Arts agreed to show painters, sculptors, and artist-decorators all together. Then, in 1901, René Guilleré set up the Société des Artistes Décorateurs; in 1903, with a remit to exhibit fine arts, architecture, and applied arts in a single venue, Frantz Jourdain founded the Salon d'Automne. Artist craftsmen, henceforth listed in the exhibition catalogs, also took part in a renaissance that was to see Emile Gallé and other "industrial artists" from Nancy, for instance, acquire first national then international renown at the various Universal Exhibitions.

These trailblazers, in striving to provide the masses with the aesthetic knowledge theretofore the preserve of an elite, were instigating "social art." Major retrospectives were organized with this intention in mind: Toulouse-Lautrec in 1904, Manet and Ingres in 1905.[6] At the Salon d'Automne in the same year, a Books and Music section was set up, paving the way for a synthesis of the arts that the following generation of creatives carried further. Influenced by the Salon d'Automne, in 1905 the Salon des Indépendants organized the first Van Gogh retrospective, and, in a fresh innovation, presented in the same venue painting, sculpture, stained glass, jewelry, as well as everyday articles.[7]

In another ground-breaking venture, in 1910 the Salon d'Automne invited the Deutscher Werkbund of Munich. The Munich group demonstrated that, thanks to a fruitful policy of industrially applied art, symbiosis between designers and industrialists was indeed feasible. It was an historic event: henceforth, however, supporters of "industrial" decorative art in France were to be labeled "German" by reaction. In 1911, the notion of staging an international exhibition for decorative and industrial arts was nevertheless mooted by Frantz Jourdain, François Carnot, president of the Union Centrale des Arts Décoratifs, Roger Sandoz, representing the French Society for the Encouragement of Art and Industry, and René Guilleré, from the Société des Artistes Décorateurs. The show itself, however, was postponed to 1925 due to World War I.

■ Facing page: Boutique René-Herbst Décoration, Alexander III Bridge, Paris, 1925 Exhibition.
Rear view of the preceding.

■ Above: Small mahogany bookcase with reading-stand, exhibited in the René-Herbst Décoration store, 1925 Exhibition. Facing page: Store-fitting, 1925 Exhibition. Influenced by Neo-Plasticism, the fittings, furniture, and lighting are by René Herbst. The gown is signed Lina Mouton.

THE ZENITH OF THE DECORATIVE ARTS

The applied arts were to attain their apogee between the years 1910 and 1920. Tabled in 1911, the Exhibition of Modern Decorative and Industrial Arts finally got off the ground in 1925, meeting with massive public success. Visitors from Paris and the provinces alike came in droves to revel in a luxurious, imaginative world, and, in particular, to gaze on the flagship pavilions, such as Jacques-Émile Ruhlmann's "Hôtel du Collectionneur," the "Musée d'Art contemporain" by the Compagnie des Arts Français (orchestrated by architect Louis Süe and painter André Mare), and the "Ambassade Française" of the Société des Artistes Décorateurs, which combined to put French interior decoration on the map. But there were others, and the lengthy list of these new *"meubliers"* (furnishers) would include Paul Follot, André Groult, Maurice Dufrêne, the decorating firm Dominique, Pierre-Paul Montagnac, Maurice Jallot, Henri Rapin, Paul Iribe, Clément Mère, as well as modern designers, like Pierre Chareau, Francis Jourdain, and Robert Mallet-Stevens whose talents were seconded and even enhanced by art craftsmen of the highest caliber who were also creators in their own right.

Some, heirs to well-established firms, had been quick to free themselves from the shackles of tradition and branch out on new paths; these were figures such as Jean Fouquet, Raymond Templier, and Gérard Sandoz, whose jewelry remains astoundingly modern. The trend surged through every area of the applied arts: fancy goods—luxury items decorated in lacquer, mother-of-pearl, or ivory—attained supremacy with Jean Dunand and Georges Bastard; sheet-metal with Claudius Linossier; ceramics with Paul Beyer, Jean Mayodon, Édouard Cazaux; glass art with René Lalique, Maurice Marinot, François Decorchemont, Daum, and Gabriel Argy-Rousseau; lighting with Perzel, Genêts, and Michon; textiles with Bianchini Férier, Hélène Henry, and Édouard Bénédictus, this last, like Da Silva Burhns, becoming renowned for carpet design. Decorating firms, such as Leleu, were flanked by designer-cum-artisans.

■ Facing page: Impressions Paul Dumas, fabric store on the Alexander III Bridge, Paris, 1925 Exhibition.

AT THE BEGINNING OF MODERNISM

THE ZENITH OF THE DECORATIVE ARTS

The period saw an abundance of talent who had at their disposal a precious palette of raw materials shipped in from the colonies: lacquer, ivory, shagreen, mother-of-pearl, ebony, palm wood, sycamore, and a spectrum of exotic timbers. The impressive roll call of designers and skilled craftsmen, together with this panoply of rare materials, turned Paris into a melting pot for design during the entire decade.

To some informed eyes, however, the success of the 1925 Exhibition, both an international event and a symbol of an era and even of a style, appeared essentially commercial. Gabriel Mourey, in the review *L'Amour de l'Art* recalled that the exhibition, though initiated by qualified professionals, had lost sight of its original objectives—"to create an inexpensive and truly democratic art,"[8] as the report of 1911 put it—owing to the predominance on the commissions and juries of representatives from industry and commerce. This "takeover" had resulted, he noted, in the erection of temporary constructions, "great barns of cardboard," a scandalous waste when a better solution would have been to construct a new district, complete with school, museum, library, underground or elevated station, with parks, avenues, cinemas and auditoriums, sports grounds, and low-cost housing to uncompromisingly utilitarian and unwaveringly modern plans.[9] Without this, the show had an old-fashioned look.

There were some notable exceptions. Robert Mallet-Stevens had planted a garden with concrete trees by sculptors Joel and Jan Martel on the esplanade of the Invalides, while the *Pavilion of Tourism* in reinforced concrete was conceived in compliance with modern-day criteria. Le Corbusier's *L'Esprit Nouveau* Pavilion, a prototype standardized "living cell" complete with garden, was, however, sidelined to the fringe of the official circuit: modern ideas were still straining to make themselves heard.

■ Pages 22–23: Hôtel Carlton, Champs-Élysées, Paris, 1933.
Facing page: Store for Siégel's, a firm specializing in shop display. Salon des Artistes Décorateurs, 1926.

■ Facing page: Pleyel piano store on the Alexander III Bridge, Paris, 1925 Exhibition. In the window a "Ruhlmann model" piano. Above: A Pleyel "Herbst model" piano, 1930. Shown at the Salon de Musique on the occasion of the first UAM Exhibition at the Musée des Arts Décoratifs.

mennequin SIÉGEL   1925 paris.

Exposition Internationale 1925. mennequin de André Vigneau. Rene. Herbst Archi Dir.

■ Two preparatory studies (black ink and color) for the Siégel store on the Alexander III Bridge, Paris, 1925. In the window, one of André Vigneau's models, dressing designed by René Herbst.
Pages 30–31: Photograph of the shopfront as realized.

une vitrine sur le pont Alexandre III_

Editeur ETAB^{ts} SIÉGEL
RENE- HERBST. A. D^r

AT THE BEGINNING
OF MODERNISM

THE INTERNATIONAL SCENE

In every country, the atmosphere was effervescent: a wholesale revolution in painting was underway, one that was to have startling repercussions on architecture and the decorative arts. Italian Futurism, born in 1909 with the publication of Marinetti's manifesto in *Le Figaro,* was forging a new aesthetic language. The group, made up of painters, sculptors, architects, poets, and musicians, extolled speed and beauty and the civilization of the machine in works dealing with the decomposition of light and dynamism. While the architect Sant'Elia was sketching plans for skyscrapers, exhibits such as that at the Galerie Bernheim in Paris in 1912, followed by others in Russia and England, fanned the flames of the international debate on modernity in artistic circles and shocked public opinion.

In France, in 1907, Picasso painted *Les Demoiselles d'Avignon,* thereby laying the foundations of Cubism. The reduction of form to geometrical elements and the abandonment of perspective were not without echoes in architecture and the applied arts. In an effort to forge a universal language for the plastic arts, De Stijl was founded in The Netherlands in 1917. An association of painters, sculptors, and architects—Piet Mondrian and Gerrit Rietveld being two key figures,—its impact on French architecture, on Robert Mallet-Stevens in particular, is undeniable. René Herbst too was tempted by this formal idiom, as witnessed by a standard lamp of a Constructivist, "Neo-Plasticist" cast presented in his store, René-Herbst Décoration, at the 1925 Exhibition.

In Germany, the Werkbund, founded in 1907 by Hermann Muthesius and the Belgian Henry Van De Velde following the example of English Arts & Crafts, was the focus of much fertile cooperation between industry and the crafts and arts. The Werkbund served as a forcing-ground for a talented generation of architects, including Peter Behrens and Walter Gropius, creator of the Bauhaus in 1919, who were busy inventing modern architecture.

■ Facing page: *Coin de Repos,* Salon d'Automne, 1921. The furniture is in gray lacquered wood underscored with green filleting. In the middle of the room, stand with a dish-shaped uplight. The white and gray pattern wallpaper matches the curtains, the folding-screen, and the upholstery on the chairs. The bow window and the alcove add an impression of space.

AT THE BEGINNING OF MODERNISM

THE INTERNATIONAL SCENE

In contact with these movements, in 1920, Le Corbusier, following a series of excursions along the shores of the Mediterranean, began publishing *L'Esprit Nouveau* in which he expounded a philosophy he materialized in a housing project of the same name that was finally erected, in the teeth of countless obstacles, at the 1925 Exhibition.

RENÉ HERBST'S EARLY CAREER

Herbst too played a part in a postwar ferment that was totally transforming the environment and creating new modes of existence. Innovation spread through artistic and industrial circles alike: architects, painters, sculptors, and illustrators worked in concert, animated by the same revolutionary spirit, turning Paris into an artistic breeding ground that endowed it with a uniquely creative atmosphere. A new age was dawning: the age of modernism.

A fresh spirit of adventure was abroad: wealth was no longer hidden out of sight, and artistic manufacture soon became synonymous with luxury. Architects and decorators joined forces with fashion designers and creators in the performing arts, providing a setting for what were new ways of living. Their ideas were presented at art events, such as the Salon d'Automne, the Salon des Artistes Décorateurs, and still more at the 1925 Exhibition—not forgetting the car and air shows, the Salon de l'Automobile and the Salon de l'Aéronautique. Already exalted by the Futurists, speed made a clamorous entrance in the shape of the automobile, which, together with electricity, was to transform street life. New means of expression appeared: novel forms such as fashion, film, the syncopated beat of jazz—each reinforced the other into a vibrant crescendo. Creators from every area and discipline were now operating in tandem. The movies offered an idealized picture of the modern interior, especially when Robert Mallet-Stevens assisted scriptwriter Marcel Lherbier on sets for movies like *L'Inhumaine* in 1923 and *Le Vertige* in 1925.

■ Facing page: *Coin de Repos*, Salon d'Automne 1921. This view of the alcove makes clear the care lavished on its details: coordinated fabrics and wallpapers, lightweight functional furniture in pastel shades.

AT THE BEGINNING
OF MODERNISM

RENÉ HERBST'S EARLY CAREER

It was not only the interest of architects that was fired by the decorative arts: couturiers too entered the fray. In 1913, Jacques Doucet disposed of his collection of eighteenth-century paintings, furniture, and objets d'art, and began assembling an extraordinary collection of modern art. In addition to setting up his legendary literature, and art and archeology library,[10] advised by André Breton (his secretary from 1919 to 1924), he purchased paintings by Braque, Picabia, and Picasso (in 1924, he acquired *Les Demoiselles d'Avignon*), as well as ordering furniture from then little-known designers such as Marcel Coard, Eileen Gray, and Pierre Legrain, the latter two being future founders of the Union des Artistes Modernes. To house these new treasures, Doucet entrusted the decoration of the interior of his studio in Neuilly to Legrain, in collaboration with the architect Paul Ruau; the result was a veritable mini-museum which the journal *L'Illustration* was to make well-known.[11] Before his death in 1929, the multi-talented Legrain also designed the UAM's insignia. Jacques Doucet passed away the same year.

The claim to fame of Paul Poiret—whose skill as a dressmaker as well as profound and wide-ranging interest in all forms of the creative arts he inherited from Doucet—was not limited to a fashion revolution which, by jettisoning the corset, was to transform the female figure. Poiret also contributed actively to the applied arts in opening a workshop dedicated to interior design, the Atelier Martine. At the 1925 Exhibition, in an original slant on this new lifestyle, he laid out his wares on three barges—christened *Amours*, *Délices*, and *Orgues*—with brightly colored interiors incorporating wall hangings, carpets, sofas, and scatter cushions, all redolent of stage sets by Bakst.

At the same 1925 Exhibition, while cabinetmakers and decorators such as Ruhlmann, Lepape, and others were occupied designing car bodies for the automobile manufacturer Delaunay-Belleville,[12] Sonia Delaunay opened a dress boutique retailing her own *tissus simultanés*. She had models pose next to the gleaming, kaleidoscopic form of an automobile

■ Pages 38–39: Cover for the book, *Devantures, vitrines, installations de magasins à l'exposition de 1925*, Éditions Charles Moreau; graphic design, René Herbst.

RENÉ HERBST'S EARLY CAREER

parked in front of Robert Mallet-Stevens' eminently futuristic *Pavilion of Tourism:* travel and speed here mixed with fashion, women's emancipation, and luxury in a heady brew.

It was in this environment that René Herbst took his first steps. His *Coin de Repos,* exhibited at the 1921 Salon d'Automne, was much remarked upon and placed him at the outset among the innovators. An architect as well as a decorator, he would restructure interior space: within it, he set up a bow window—an architectural element borrowed from Northern Europe—and an alcove in which the furniture (console-bookshelf, settee, corner-cabinet) was embedded to make the most of the limited space. Designed to hold books, curios, and plants, his furniture fulfills all the requirements of a living room, in the literal sense of the word, and yet does away with clutter. The room feels spacious and convivial, with highly finished gray enamel furniture adorned in green fillets, a ceiling underscored by a cornice, and walls lined with wallpaper in a white pattern over a gray ground that coordinates with the folding-screen and reps upholstery on the armchairs. A freestanding column bears a dish-shaped light.

The *Coin de Repos* stands at the junction between the art of interior designers, who were preaching attention to detail, and that of those architects of the modern movement who, from the 1920s on, were concerning themselves increasingly with the "minimum dwelling" and so invading wall surfaces to free up the interior space. In this respect, Herbst's work stems from investigations initiated in France by Francis Jourdain, whom he rightly considered as the doyen of his generation, with his interchangeable[13] furniture (only the chairs and tables were moveable, the other pieces being fixed to the walls) presented at the Salon d'Automne in 1913 which was to be greeted with approbation by Le Corbusier.

1. *L'Industriel Savoisien* (April 1, 1933). **2**. Laurence Graffin, *André Mare. Carnets de guerre 1914–1918* (Herscher, 1996). **3**. *André Mare. Cubisme et camouflage,* exhibition in Bernay, Paris, and Brussels in 1998. **4**. *La Psychologie et la Vie* (December 1936). **5**. Frantz Jourdain, "La décoration et le réalisme architecturaux à l'Exhibition de 1889," *La Revue des arts décoratifs* (1889), quoted in Arletté Barré-Despond and Suzanne Tise, *Jourdain* (Paris: Le Regard, 1988). **6**. Ibid., p. 99. **7**. Ibid., p. 105. **8**. Gabriel Mourey, "L'esprit de l'exhibition," *L'Amour de l'Art,* (1925). **9**. Gabriel Mourey quoted by Yvonne Brunhammer, *Le Beau dans l'utile,* 1925, p. 33. **10**. The Bibliothèque littéraire d'art et d'archéologie was presented to the City of Paris in 1918. **11**. André Joubin, "Le Studio de Jacques Doucet," *L'Illustration* (May 3, 1930). **12**. *Bulletin de la vie artistique,* no. 9 (May 1, 1925). **13**. Barré-Despond and Tise, *Jourdain* (Paris: Le Regard, 1988, p. 252).

DEVANTVRES VITRINES INSTALLATIONS DE MAGASINS

A L'

EXPOSITION INTERNATIONALE DES ARTS DECORATIFS

PARIS 1925

H

DITEVR

C.H

IOREAV

II RVE DE

RAGVE

ARIS XII

STAGING
MODERN ART

2

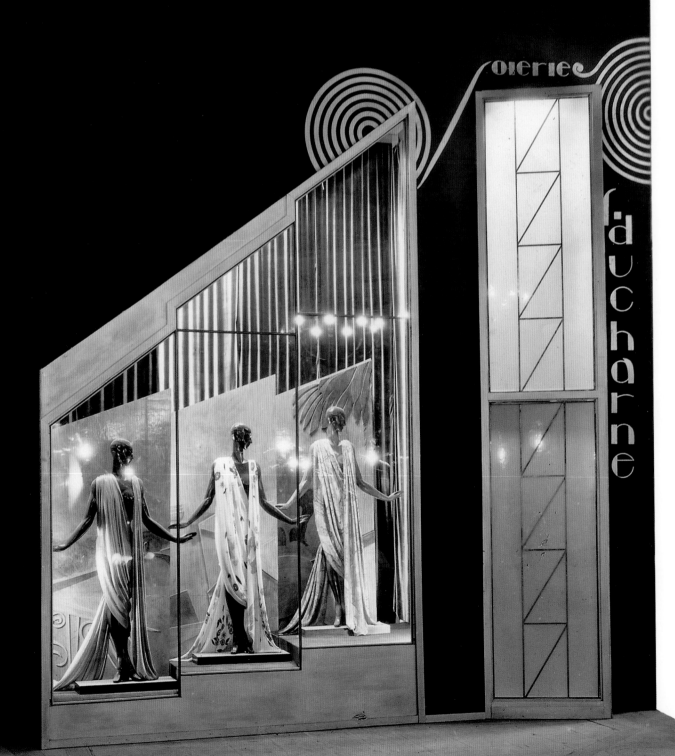

DECORATING THE STREET

"René Herbst, a modest figure, does not like to shout the merits of his furniture from the roof tops. He is proud, however, and with good reason, of his role as a creator in the art of store display. . . . The fairylike charm of window dressing started out with René Herbst. Before him, there was nothing." HENRI CLOUZOT[1]

René Herbst was convinced that the "art of the street" was the best way to open the public mind to modernity. "By taking decoration into the street," he pronounced, "one could turn our modern cities into real open-air museums. The public will learn much from a décor [that is] the daily companion of its walks through the streets."[2]

It is true that the success of modernism was to owe much to art in an urban environment. The mindset of the population at large was not averse to modernization in the street: pedestrians, after admiring shiny automobiles and all the conveniences of urban furniture, such as benches, newspaper kiosks, and street lighting, were now to stand agog before sumptuously lit window displays. Street life was further enlivened by neon signs and advertising billboards, which, thanks to talents of the caliber of Cassandre, Charles Loupot, and Jean Carlu, were treated as artistic disciplines in their own right. The street became a platform for modernity: on the instigation of forward-thinking minds such as Robert Mallet-Stevens and Francis Jourdain, urban art now made its entrance into the official Salons.

In 1922, the Salon d'Automne showcased an "urban art" section, being followed shortly afterwards by the Salon des Artistes Décorateurs. René Herbst was of course an early exhibitor. In 1923, he joined the group show of boutiques at the Salon d'Automne, where the main contributors included Francis Jourdain, Robert Mallet-Stevens, and Pierre Chareau. The event marked the beginning of some lifelong friendships. On the occasion of the 1924 Salon d'Automne, the great hall of the Grand Palais was converted into a

■ Page 41: Storefront for Ducharne silks, Salon d'Automne 1926. Pages 42, 43, and 45: Three projects for the firm of Siégel, including window dressing, shopfront (boulevard Haussmann, Paris, 1930), and a color drawing showing the store published in *Devanture de boutique*, Éditions Charles Moreau.

public space featuring ten shops: a bookshop, a jeweler's, a clothing outlet, a store for ceramics and interiors—supplemented by an array of street furniture—newspaper kiosk, phone booth, bus shelter, and a bench and two fountains, signed by Robert Mallet-Stevens. As project superintendent, he had called on the collaboration of René Herbst, Francis Jourdain, Gabriel Guevrekian, Djo-Bourgeois, Rigault, Nathan, Jean Burckhalter, Paul Poiret, Pierre Chareau, and Le Même. In the same Salon, under the Siégel label, René Herbst exhibited a boutique of his own, with dresses by Madeleine Vionnet, shoes by Perugia, and outfits by Crabette. Critics dubbed the store "ultramodern." Then, at the 1925 International Exhibition, Herbst presented five luxury shops on the Alexander III Bridge: fashion was represented by Madeleine Vionnet, industry by the shop-display firm Siégel, pianos by Pleyel, textiles by Dumas, and liqueurs by Cusenier; interior decoration featured Herbst's own store, René-Herbst Décoration.

THE ART OF STORE DISPLAY

For René Herbst, everything starts with the art of display, the linchpin of the ideas he was to defend throughout his career. For Herbst, a store display is a stage set where, in a suitable architectural space, lighting is used to enhance the product. His plans and contributions to the Salons set the tone. Press cuttings gathered by Herbst himself and preserved in his archives are instructive in this regard, since the occasionally meticulous descriptions of the works and the commentaries they contain help one relive these now historic events. The 1923 Artistes Décorateurs was the scene of one of his finest achievements, a store for the boot-maker Perugia, himself considered a master of his trade. His dazzlingly luxurious shoes, made from cloth of gold and ornamental leather, were presented by Herbst "as artworks."[3] The store, "in red and green tones underscored by golden filleting,"[4] was deliberately calculated to draw the eye to the items on sale.

■ Salon des Artistes Décorateurs, 1926. Fashion boutiques presented in a sawtooth arrangement, and featuring dresses by Callot, Jenny, Worth, and Lanvin, with mannequins by André Vigneau manufactured by Siégel's.

THE ART OF STORE DISPLAY

"As much skill has been exercised here as in the design of a doorway or a jewel," art critic Yvanohé Rambosson exclaimed. The wares themselves were characterized as the "unreal shoes of Master Perugia."[5] The store, noted Léandre Vaillat in *Le Temps*, "holds the promise of an aesthetic of the street." The frontage was that of a palace exposing its brilliantly lit interior to the sidewalk. In the center, a single display shelf with shoes was reflected in mirrors to the sides surmounted by a mural decoration. In the windows, "pillar units bore elegant ankle boots on sheets of glass."[6] The splendid photographs of the store capture an astonishing realization whose modernity remains undiminished.

In 1927, appointed art director for the shop display firm of Siégel's, Herbst founded the trade journal, *Parade.*[7] The frankly didactic articles amount to a course of continuing education, and describe, with the aid of sketches, the best displays for product, with, in particular, a systematic method of balancing masses so as to obtain the most striking effect and thus "hook" the shopper-to-be. The informative and wide-ranging text was seconded by examples of projects from many nations. Competitions were organized. As was his habit, René Herbst spent lavishly; there followed no less than ten issues devoted to window dressing, shop display, and store interiors. Starting out from the commodity itself, Herbst developed a veritable science that he went on to promote in writing:

"Laying merchandise out does not mean piling it up any old how. One has—and this is imperative—one has to build a display as one would build a house. One needs plans and elevations, one has to research the materials, colors, and lighting—everything plays its own part in the construction of the sales display."[8]

To do this, he declared: "When about to embark on a store, the architect has immediately to think about the window dressing and bear in mind that the surround has to become invisible beneath the display structure." Inserted within a specially designed architectural space, the store window has above all "to combine volume, color, lighting."

■ Inside the Siégel store on boulevard Haussmann, Paris, 1931. The lighting and chromium-plated metal points up various architectural elements, such as the cornice, shop window, banister, and wall lamp.

COQUEMER

SIEGEL

CARRON sœurs

les parfums de rosine

paul poiret
THE

N° 31
15 JUILLET 1929

"PARADE"

REVUE DU DÉCOR

DE LA RUE

TROISIÈME ANNEE

■ Facing page: Detail of the *Shopping street* at the Salon des Artistes Décorateurs, 1927. "10 cleverly lit storefronts, arranged fanwise due to the limited space, presenting luxury goods, and adjoining a hotel lobby." *Paris-Soir.* Above: *Parade, revue du décor de la rue*, no. 31, 1929; René Herbst was the art director on the review from 1927 through 1937. Pages 52–53: Inside Henriette Léon's handbag store, 1928. "A veritable revolution, a living art, the bags seem as if suspended, the supports invisible."

CARRON SŒURS

■ Pages 54 and 55: Carron Sœurs store, 129, boulevard Haussmann, Paris. Design for the storefront and interior of the boutique. Above: Cover for the book, *Nouvelles devantures et agencements de magasins parisiens*, Éditions Charles Moreau, 1933, presenting the Luminex storefront, 1929. Graphic design, R. Herbst. Facing: View of the interior decoration for the Luminex outlet.

THE ART OF STORE DISPLAY

To stop passersby in their tracks, "a 'scene-display' has to be easy to understand—this is the architect's job." Accessories play a major role in this connection, and so Herbst set himself to restyling these too. Breaking with tradition, he had made silhouette dummies in wood, in copper wire, and later even in glass. After an initial trial for drapery by Madeleine Vionnet at the Salon des Artistes Décorateurs, he experimented further with the firm of Siégel and, at Galeries Lafayette, presented his first cut-out display dummies for men in 1923 and for women in 1924. These wooden cut-outs were furnished with mobile and interchangeable heads and arms. As against traditional wax mannequins, which look stiff and straitlaced, his "unreal mannequins," as he dubbed them, reproduced only the body's outline to improve the visibility of the outfit or fabric on sale. He also observed that only department stores are at liberty to change their displays indefinitely. "The frontage of a department store resembles a theater set in which everything should be removable." To facilitate changes in décor, the ceiling should allow for the fitting of any system of fixed or mobile lighting required without damage; the flooring should feature dismountable elements; the sides and rear, neutral in tone, have to be readily accessible to enable the display to be fine-tuned. But, as Herbst insists, a store window cannot hope to exist without lighting. Reflectors make it possible to either focus rays on a particular area or illuminate in depth, though they have to be supplemented by pencil beams that, converging at a point, highlight the star attraction of the display. "The lighting should pleasantly bathe a shop window without drawing attention to its source." It is moreover imperative to integrate into the windows aeration systems designed by lighting engineers, to render less unbearable the blazing heat and stifling air under the intense illumination. Lastly, Herbst even suggests making the storefront actually move by projecting films:

"There is certainly much to be done in window dressing by use of moving pictures that will form an integral part of the setting [and bring] an original touch to the decoration of the street."[9]

■ Pages 59 and 60–61: Shop for Perugia, shoemaker, Salon des Artistes Décorateurs, 1923. Facade (p. 59) and interior view (p. 60–61): "The shoes are presented like artworks." *Revue des Beaux-Arts.*
Pages 62–63: International Exhibition of Arts and Techniques, Paris, 1937; Charles Moreau, publisher, Jean Luce, tableware and settings, and Jean Puiforcat, silverware, at the Centre des Métiers d'Art.

chaussures

RENÉ HERBST DECORATION FOR THE STREET

With a diversity of displays showing products from all branches of human activity, the street is not just somewhere for the blandishments of advertising; it is also a museum, in which a passerby might come to finish his education.

The street's dual role, the interest of which is increasingly accepted in the modern era, should bring with it rapid developments in the art of presentation.

The numerous hoardings spilling out over our sidewalks are sufficient proof of the drive for ever-changing storefronts; retailers have understood that goods, whatever their nature, have to be artistically presented to be appealing. The public, following experiments that at first tended to frighten it off, has adapted to the situation; one might even say that it is because of urban art that it has begun little by little to take to the modern taste. The hoardings themselves are no more a fence of disjointed boards as in former times, but temporary shop windows in which a tradesman can continue to exhibit his merchandise (an innovation we owe to René Prou).

Plastered with posters, these billboards make an agreeable splash—especially when signed Cassandre, Carlu, or Loupot, etc. The stores of yesteryear, without style (I do not think that one can call ghastly fascias in the Louis XV and XVI mode, "style"), and with their out-of-date surrounds, now stick out like sore thumbs among those made by the architects and decorators of our own time. As this dynamic art continues to evolve, one can clearly discern a general tendency to

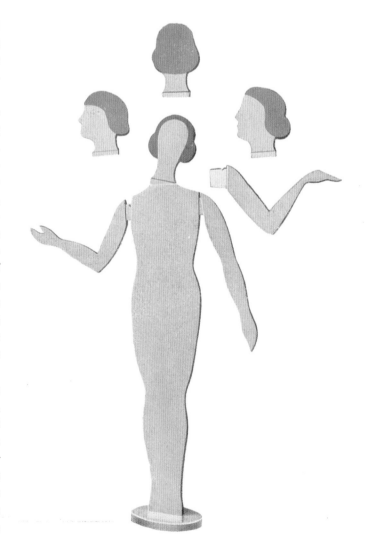

simplification of form and line; it seems that the shop is rightly considered a backdrop in which excess decoration might perhaps excite the interest of passers-by, but only to distract them from the basic aim of the exercise: displaying the commodity. At the risk of repeating myself, and the reader will have to excuse me, artists must take a stand against the overuse of such frontages in one and the same building. The architect who designs a storefront is obliged to impose its environment on the stores' occupants; our artists are well capable of ironing out this problem while offering a personal slant on their allotted task.

This is why the art of the window dresser [in France] has undergone such progress in recent years; it is he who makes stores endlessly inviting, as much through his style as by the ingenuity of his displays. The whole store must be conceived and fitted out in such manner as to allow him to make the most of the goods on show.

Lighting, the selection and siting of appliances, play a key role and a display cannot be perfect without rational but not blinding lighting that suitably emphasizes the product. Fortunately, there are lighting engineers to assist architect and decorator, since the latter, no matter how talented, can never equal the skill of a specialist. Their collaboration is imperative: the calculation of a curve, the positioning of a lamp or some other apparatus has nothing to do with aesthetics, and a technician must find its correct shape and location—nothing can be left to chance. In America, where lighting plays an enormous role, they have not yet grasped its true value. Admittedly, the intensity is formidable, the lamps almost touch, but the crucial point—the interplay of light and shade—seems to escape them. In France, where electricity is distributed more parsimoniously, dosage is the key, and, in these conditions, window dressers here face a more delicate task.

Yet hasn't Mallet-Stevens shown the way in his most recent creations, (Bally and the Café du Brésil)? There, the lighting met with total success thanks to the assistance of an engineer, M. Solomon.

Like the preceding, the present book, the fourth series, has, as far as possible, set its sights on eclecticism, and, among the many recent achievements by architects and decorators, we have chosen those that most closely correspond to the general trends I have just outlined. These are joined by a number of documents from abroad, providing a more rounded picture.

RENÉ-HERBST
New window dressings and store display
Introduced by René Herbst 4th series. C. Moreau

■ Wooden cut-out store dummy with interchangeable head and arms, used mainly for displaying fabrics for dresses and coats. "Complete with head, body, and two selected arms. Extra spare parts." Advertising brochure, c. 1924. Manufacturers Siégel, design René Herbst.

ET INSTALL

DEVANTURES

MAG

ÉDITIONS D'ART CHARLES

ATIONS
E

ASINS

AU, 8, RUE DE PRAGUE, PARIS-XII

RENÉ HERBST STORE DISPLAY

One can distinguish two sorts of display:
1) for retailers
2) for hawkers, who place their merchandise on the public thoroughfare.

The former cannot encroach on the highway without a special permit from the town council; the latter are subject to general measures that the same authorities think fit to impose regulating them. . . .

Did the Phoenicians, the foremost merchants of Antiquity—dubbed, "the Englishmen of the Ancient World"—know how to display goods? Yes. They used displays, laying out and exposing their goods before the intended purchaser. . . .

For the medieval period, allow us to quote the words of Monsieur Clouzot in his book, *Présentation* (1927), where, in a most illuminating foreword, he traces the history of display. The Middle Ages took place in an emporium without external doors lit by a vast bay opening at waist height on whose ledge the goods were laid out, or suspended above it. One did not have to enter to make a purchase . . . Display already existed. . . . By the eighteenth century little had altered; however, clear glass was making an appearance and it was now possible to view merchandise from outside. The great changes date from the nineteenth century, with the introduction of the sidewalk that allowed tradesmen to present their goods to greater advantage. Lighting too entered service at that time, an essential factor in store windows. Without lighting, a display cannot sell. . . .

We swiftly come to the twentieth century, in which we can appreciate the massive strides made in window display. As Maurice Dufrène has said: "Barely ten years ago, it didn't even exist." No true artist, professional or otherwise, had applied himself to the question—none had as yet "shown his wares." . . .

To attract by an idea, by lighting, by a new style of layout, to hold the attention by the detail and quality of this style . . . that's the point—to attract and retain—for, to retain is to win over, and to win over means to sell.

In effect, laying merchandise out does not mean piling it up any old way. One has—and this is imperative—one has to build a display as one would build a house You need plans and elevations, you have to research materials, colors, and lighting—everything plays its part in the construction of the sales display.

A coarse expression, perhaps, "sales display"; the point one has to remember is that the tradesman wishes above all to liquidate his goods. It is the merchandise and not the accessory that has to come first. It is the "star." (It is understood that I am speaking here solely about sales displays and not advertising displays.) . . .

It is for this reason that, when about to embark on a store fitting, an architect ought immediately to think about the window dressing and bear in mind that its framework has to become invisible beneath the display structure. This is how to show goods at their best. Naturally, a frontage has to suit the merchandise too. A jeweler's window cannot have the same proportions as a tailor's or grocer's; the lighting will be different as well. . . . The window has to possess the right proportions. More especially, passersby must not be forced to lift or lower their heads to see the lead article. The eye of the pedestrian—the intended purchaser—has to be caught immediately, without obstacles of any kind; he has to be beguiled and captivated quickly, without having to indulge in gymnastics to admire the article or see its price.

Moreover, shoppers have to be able to rapidly locate the article, if it is impossible to view it in-store. To do this, it is necessary that the window be set up correctly, that the "scene-display" be easy to understand—this is the architect's job. . . .

Large-scale sales displays have to contain a certain number of goods, in symmetrical or asymmetrical compositions. Just because there is a significant number of articles does not mean that the window dresser is to align or lay them out haphazardly on the accessories.

■ Pages 66–67: Cover of the book, *Devantures et installations de magasins,* Éditions Charles Moreau.
Graphic design René Herbst.
Facing page: Store design for Isabey perfumes at the Salon d'Automne, 1927.

RENÉ HERBST STORE DISPLAY

One needs, above all, to combine volume, color, lighting, so as to obtain, in spite of its uniformity, that glimmer of interest that will stop the passerby. . . .

Accessories play a crucial role in display. There are two kinds: metal or wooden accessories that can be used indefinitely and lend themselves to a thousand combinations in presenting articles (to enhance the item they should be almost completely invisible), and decorative accessories, a temporary accompaniment to the merchandise, made out of less durable material, and, most importantly, of lower cost.

Such accessories have a place in stores where the displays can be changed frequently and are used to liven up the presentations. Silhouettes cut out of wood, metal components, decoration, etc.

The "unreal" shop dummy made a discreet appearance but little by little they are replacing the hideous wax heads, perfect imitations of nature, mannequins for the Musée Grévin [wax museum] which have no place in modern window dressing. . . .

A few years ago, in 1921, I had the idea that, decoration being irrelevant, it might be possible to display dresses or fabrics on a silhouette cut out of a plank of wood. In 1924, Madeleine Vionnet presented drapery on just such a silhouette at the Salon des Artistes Décorateurs.

I went on to employ copper wire for the silhouettes to convey an idea of the accessory's purpose. Today, such figures are everywhere.

Before addressing advertising displays, those for department stores have to be treated separately. Possessing enormous windows, they are able to vary their displays indefinitely. Department store windows are a stage set where everything can be dismantled. . . .

As we understand it, a department store window should have the largest dimensions available, though it should be possible, depending on the articles displayed, to reduce it by use of removable interior components. It should, in particular, measure at least 8 ft. 2 in. (2.50 m) to 9 ft. 8 in. (3 m) deep.

The ceiling should be capable of being fitted with any system of fixed or mobile lighting without damage; the flooring should feature dismountable elements; the sides and rear, neutral in tone, like all the visible areas of the window, can be equipped with decorations and curtains as required. Moreover, at least two access points (to the rear and sides) should be included for fine-tuning the display. Lastly, dadoes should not exceed one to one and a half feet (30 to 40 cm).

Department stores have had little hesitation in entrusting their displays to young artists (to date, displays had been constructed on the premises, by shifts of employees from the given departments). The effect has been virtually immediate and, for the public, our stores have become an object of curiosity where good taste, in conjunction with sumptuous materials, turns windows into genuine works of art.

We readily acknowledge that it is thanks to department stores that window display has evolved so rapidly since the war.

In the future, advertising display will become preponderant; it is this the public understands best, that strikes it quickest, that wins it over most immediately.

What is an advertising display? It is an architectural or decorative composition in which retail product is shown to its best advantage: it is initially this architectural or decorative composition that strikes, attracts, and charms the viewer. The article on sale is in fact secondary—it is there, but will be seen by pedestrians only because the decoration pulls them in.

The advertising display is a poster in relief. Not too much text (passersby read little). Brand name, trademark, a pithy slogan, price tag, and that's it.

The Germans and the Dutch are especially fond of this mode of display. They build like architects; with them, one never encounters wood or copper accessories, permanent accessories.

Over there, everything is centered on advertising; they are architects rather than decorators. No futile décor—volumes, planes, colors. Their displays present better than ours; their execution is inferior in terms of finish, but that's not the point: it's income that matters. They employ colored paper, plywood: they manage to play with light skillfully (it's true that they possess superior materials to us). Industrialists in those nations put considerable emphasis on display.

Department stores aside, most of the time in France we are faced with a paltry little display that answers to no particular purpose and which is to some degree the cause of much business slipping through our fingers. . . .

Street decoration and the attraction and interest this decoration contributes to the sidewalk have made our modern cities into genuine open-air museums. The public learns much from a décor that it sees every day, the daily companion of its walks through our streets. . . .

As we previously stated, a shop window cannot exist without lighting. In a department store, both fixtures and mobile components are employed. Inside the surrounds of the bay are fitted with electric sockets; the sources of power for the lamps cannot be more than 3 ft. 3 in. (1 m) away.

Two types of reflecting apparatus are deployed: the first type, intensifying reflectors, allows light rays to be focused on a given spot; the second type, depth [*attractifs*] reflectors, allows lighting at greater depth. Such settings might make great use of small lamps with concentrating reflectors, as well as floodlights with color filters.

Some make beams converge at a single location without, however, casting shadows on the window; others, of high intensity, shine a pencil of light concentrated at a point . . . Sometimes, in the upper zones,

RENE HERBST STORE DISPLAY

fixed intensive reflectors are embedded in formwork invisible to the public. Occasionally, small, concentric spotlights can be used to illuminate the "star" article.

The lighting should pleasantly bathe a shop window without drawing attention to its source. Many stores flood their windows with excessive light: without shadows, the relief disappears, and, due to the brightness, all attraction practically evaporates: by dint of this, selling power is reduced markedly.

In my opinion, relief is an absolute necessity. Lighting a figure too brightly totally deprives it of character; consequently, window dressers and decorators have gradually had to become lighting engineers, honing their designs, placing articles advantageously, and endowing them with the desired "set-attraction" [attrait-scène].

It should not be forgotten that mechanical power is another necessity, and that one relies on it either to impart rotary movement or else for films in many displays. Cinema has made an entrance solely on screens on which various scenes can be projected. There is certainly much to be done in window dressing with the use of moving pictures that will form an integral part of the setting. I have, furthermore, seen some truly sensational and to my mind conclusive experiments: these too will soon be employed in display,

bringing an original touch to street decoration. Developments in store display have also stimulated the interest of our modern engineers. One area of their expertise, ventilation, is a field in which they have brought great improvements. In effect, the brightness of the lights was making the air inside the windows unbreathable. Wax mannequins melted and one could even see these hideous heads, their faded make-up oozing [traces] of wax, their features completely distorted, offering a horrible mask to the public gaze.

Aeration is no insignificant factor. In-store and window-display ventilation are closely interrelated; in terms of execution, today's merchandisers are real marvels. In Holland, one department store has entirely mechanized its displays. Assembled on elevators, the displays are constantly made up in the basement and rapidly assembled in situ without inconveniencing the public in the slightest. Any window dressing can be assembled or altered in less than ten minutes. . . .

Let us not forget that it is by the decoration of its streets that a country is judged. It is impossible to overstate the importance of a constantly changing aspect of the urban fabric that constitutes its very life—its window displays.

RENÉ-HERBST
Handwritten text, René Herbst archives

■ Mounting metal components for OTUA, International Exhibition, Johannesburg, 1958.

■ Above: René Herbst at the International Exhibition of Arts and Techniques in Modern Life, Paris 1937.
Plan of the exhibition and site of its 10,000 m² installation: Centre des Métiers d'Art, the Advertising
Pavilion and the UAM Pavilion. Graphic document devised by René Herbst.
Facing page: Rubafer Stand, Maubeuge iron founders at the 1937 Exhibition; display design by René Herbst.

MILLE METRES DE LONG

RUBAFER

FABRIQUE
DE FER DE
MAUBEUGE

TOLES

EXHIBITION DESIGN

As a past master in the art of shop display, it was natural for René Herbst to turn his hand to exhibition design. At the exhibitions of urban art at the 1926 and 1927 Salons des Artistes Décorateurs, he had proved himself capable of more than fashion boutiques and luxury stores. Pursuing this new path, among other innovations, he deployed sets of mirrors and built-in integral lighting, and dressed windows in sawtooth- and fan-shapes in the way of a giant kaleidoscope. In 1930, for the debut exhibition of the avant-garde French movement, the Union des Artistes Modernes, he erected his own *Salon de Musique* on a sloping, black floor to increase visual impact—a device to which he reverted at the 1931 Salon d'Automne. His reputation for setting up exhibitions was further enhanced on dealing with heavy industry, first in 1929 at the International Exhibition at Liège, and then, in 1931, at the Colonial Exhibition in Paris. There, as Henri Clouzot describes, "he juggled blocks of granite, steel coils, and building frames with the same ease as he might a parure of brilliants or a pearl necklace in a [jeweler's] window on the rue de la Paix."[10] Such feats were repeated at the Brussels Exhibition of 1935, when Herbst presented "a colossal and cleverly arranged sheaf of metallurgical components in their raw state, sheets, beams, etc., that flaunt the sheer beauty of the raw material."[11]

Keenly interested in both radio and cinema, he had already suggested projecting films in window displays, and, at the 1928 Salon de la Radiophonie, he set up a broadcasting studio in which visitors could speak into a microphone and sound-test their voice. In Brussels in 1935, he presented a design for a movie theater in which the center of attraction would be the eye-catching glass partitions around the projectionist's cabin. "Man and machine together form a living decor," he explained.[12] Hired by the Office Technique d'Utilisation de l'Acier (OTUA) to publicize iron and steel and the metal industries generally on the occasion of the international exhibitions, Herbst was consequently at the same time contributor to and exhibit designer for events that resonated worldwide.[13]

■ Pages 76–77: Advertising Pavilion, interior, 1937 Exhibition. The architecture was to have been allotted to Herbst, but it was completed by official architects taking their cue from plans by Herbst. Interior display design by Herbst with Jean Carlu. At the rear, a poster for the liner *Normandie* by Cassandre.
Facing page: Visitors to the 1937 Exhibition sitting in steel-tubing chairs designed by René Herbst.

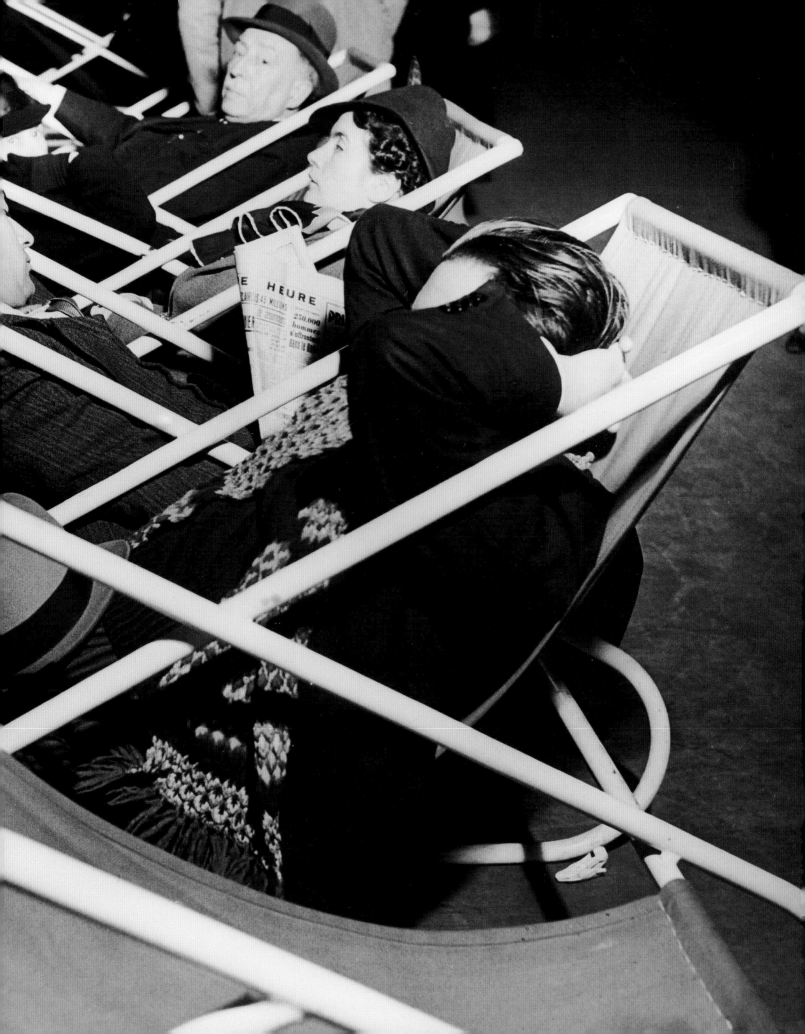

EXHIBITION DESIGN

From Liège in 1929 to Moscow in 1961, Herbst covered thousands of square meters on themes such as iron and steel, metallurgy, electricity, and the graphic arts.

After the war, he further broadened his scope as an arranger of exhibitions with a range of artistic and industrial events, such as the annual *Formes Utiles* staged in the Grand Palais under the auspices of the Salon des Arts Ménagers, the Milan Triennials, for which he headed the French contingent in 1954, 1957, and 1960, as well as exhibits in the Musée des Arts Décoratifs in which he took an active part.[14]

SELECT AND PERSUADE

By now an authority in the field, after World War II, René Herbst accelerated these activities, focusing on exhibitions dedicated to a vast range of themes. Questioned on this very subject,[15] Herbst remarked that there are two main categories of exhibition: pedagogic ones that treat their subject in the round, and those of commercial or industrial nature where the brief is to present models and appliances. He aspired to maximum simplicity, but steered clear of austerity. In so doing, he generally deployed two complementary methods of presentation: vertical display used as a signal, while documents are presented horizontally. "One cannot say everything in an exhibition, one has to make a choice," he advised. "The means deployed to give prominence to the objects exposed include light, movement, graphics, soundtracks, and film projection. In addition, I am always on the lookout for the telling detail that allows the best to be brought out in an exhibit, be it a commodity or a valuable document." And, standing by his modernist principles, Herbst concluded: "For, one cannot prove anything or convince anyone by accumulation, only by selection."

■ Pages 80 and 81: Two interior views of the UAM Pavilion, 1937 Exhibition, built by G. H. Pingusson with F.-P. Jourdain and A.-L. Louis. The glass-fronted construction runs parallel to the Seine. One notes René Herbst's stands (p. 80) with, in the foreground, steel and wicker furniture, and, behind, his multipurpose studio furniture (see also p. 137). Facing page: Printing and graphic arts Section; design, René Herbst (see also p. 177).

1. Henri Clouzot, *L'Industriel Savoisien* (April 1, 1933). 2. *Store Display*, René Herbst Archives, p. 68–73 of present work. 3. *Revue des Beaux-Arts*. 4. René Chavance, *Art et Décoration*. 5. *Paris Midi*. 6. Chavance, *Art et Décoration*. 7. He directed the review *Parade* for ten years from 1927 to 1937. 8. *Store Display*, Archives, p. 68–73 of present work. 9. Ibid. 10. Henri Clouzot, *L'Industriel Savoisien*. 11. Renée Moutard-Uldry, *Beaux-Arts* (April 26, 1935). 12. Ibid. 13. See the Chronology, p. 206–213 of the present work. 14. First exhibition of *Formes Utiles* in 1949, the French contemporary art Triennial in 1956, *Vie Quotidienne* in 1962, and *Formes Industrielles* in 1963. 15. René Herbst interviewed by Y. Jenger in *Cahiers de l'Association des amis du musée pédagogique*, no. 4 (June 1957).

■ Pages 85 and 86: *Art and Advertising in the World* show organized by the Alliance Graphique Internationale
(AGI), at the Musée des Arts Décoratifs, 1955. Interior view (p. 85) and entrance to the show.
Above: International Exhibition, Johannesburg, 1958. Exhibition display construction for OTUA. Photograph altered
by René Herbst. Pages 88–89: René Herbst's last large-scale achievement, the OTUA Pavilion, Moscow, 1961.

PIONEER
OF A NEW STYLE

3

FAUTEUIL LÉGER TUBES & TISSUS

FURNITURE

"In addition to the old duet of wood and stone, which we have never neglected, we have also attempted to assemble a harmonious quartet featuring cement, glass, metal, and electricity." UAM *Manifesto*[1]

René Herbst designed furniture, as he fitted out interiors, to fulfill a need and never out of a desire for decoration. He did not try to impose the same style on every project, but placed himself instead at the service of the aim in view. Firmly of the opinion that the sole function of furniture is to be used, he constantly reiterated Francis Jourdain's remark to the effect that "furniture should not resemble intrusive and talkative visitors, but discreet servants who know how not to waylay us with their quaintly eccentric attire or unwarranted eloquence. The only statement to be tolerated on the part of an armchair is an invitation to repose."[2] An inventory of the forms Herbst created amply demonstrates the eclecticism he was to embrace in the field of furniture.[3] Store display, an activity on which he lavished great care, had induced him to adapt interior spaces by use of sectioned walls, mirrors, and built-in lighting, as can be seen, for example, in the Charon and Isabey stores; he also had to design furniture—from tables and chairs to occasional pieces and display units which, to achieve their purpose, were necessarily functional, even minimalist. For both Perugia's shoes (1923) and Henriette Léon's bags (1928), he deployed "invisible" (i.e., translucent) supports, which made the items on display appear "unreal,"[4] like sculptures. For Robj's objets d'art (1927), he devised small-sized wall modules and display elements in black-varnished wood, the lines underscored with a metal armature, and, for Madeleine Vionnet (1925), vitrine-tables in wood and clear glass or marble. Keeping the goal uppermost in mind, he would employ expensive materials for luxury stores but, for a company like Luminex, he would use instead industrial stock, such as metal and glass, which might also serve for demonstration.

■ Page 91: Ceiling lamp for the Aga Khan dining-room. Pages 92–93: Dining room for Léonce Rosenberg, Paris, 1929, with furniture by Herbst, sculpture by J. Csaky, paintings by G. Valmier, and stained glass by L. Barillet and J. Le Chevallier. Page 94: Entrance of an apartment for M. Peissi, managing director of OTUA. Page 95: Drawing from a notebook by Herbst. The metal-tubing chair, made for Rosenberg, was upholstered in leather (see p. 92–93).

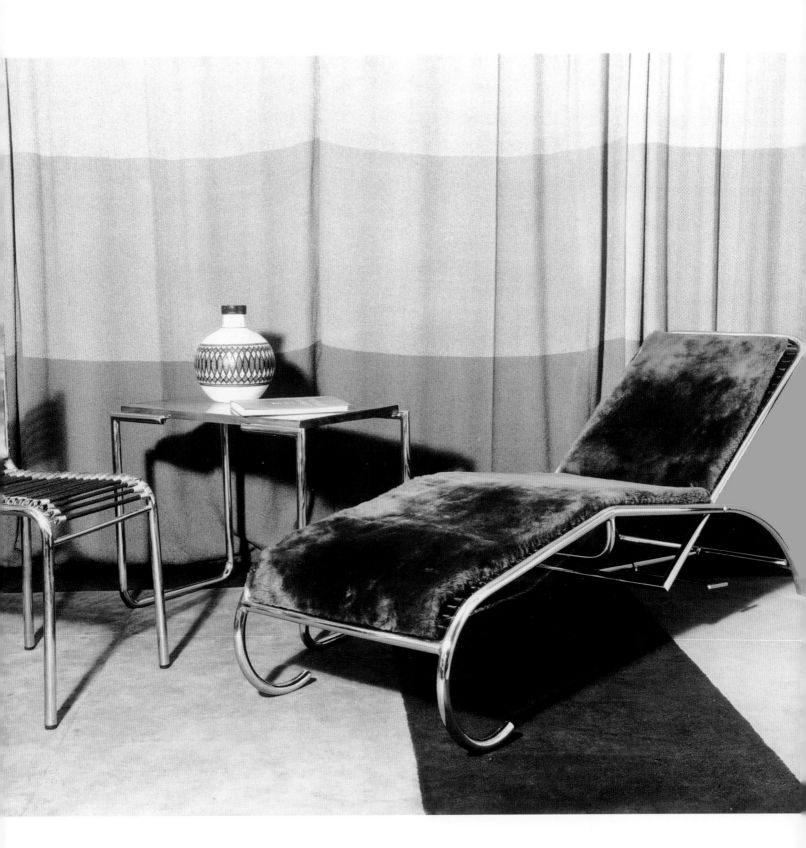

In setting up stands for Jean Luce (table settings), Jean Puiforcat (goldsmith), Charles
Moreau (publisher), and the OTUA (application of steel) at the 1937 Exhibition, he was
forever adapting his approach to suit the exhibitor. With private commissions, he could
experiment and enjoy a creative freedom and an open-mindedness often missing in the
industrial and commercial arenas. The furniture he conceived for the art dealer Rosenberg
in 1929 betrays no parallels in the French *ébénisterie* tradition: the pier elements, consoles,
seats, and tables are in metal, leather, and glass, and there are the elastic strap seat bottoms
for which he became celebrated.

His most prestigious order was for the Aga Khan's private residence, rue Scheffer in
Paris. The commission covered architectural restoration, interior refit, and furniture design,
and was to stretch over three years from 1930 to 1933. Herbst was to exhibit a great deal
of furniture from this account: the rosewood and chromium-plated metal dining room at
the Galerie Georges-Petit,[5] the startling dressing table for the princess in glass and metal at
the Musée des Arts Décoratifs,[6] the bureau-bookcase for the prince himself, made of
mahogany and nickel-plated steel, at the Musée Galliera,[7] photographs of the entire renovation at the Galerie Renaissance[8] and also at the Salon d'Automne in the course of which
he was also able to display a gaming table complete with chairs,[9] and, finally, the exhibition
of French decorative art at the Galerie Bernheim-Jeune that gave him the opportunity of
showing the mahogany and chromium-plated metal *bahut-vaisselier* (Welsh dresser or sideboard).[10] In an interview in *Le Figaro illustré* on the subject of the future of wood faced with
such competition from metal, marble, and plastic, Herbst reiterated his interest in every
material and explained his choices for the Aga Khan commission:

"Metals and all the plastics have not killed off wood. Wood will always find a place
in certain interiors. I am currently involved in decorating a private mansion and the
idea of using metal did not enter my head for a second. Steel is good in its place, but

■ Page 97: Metal suite created c. 1930 including a velvet-covered *chaise longue*, a rubber-strap seat and
an occasional table. Pages 98–99: *Dining room and corner in a hall*, Salon d'Automne, 1931, presented
as window dressing on inclined planes: "A 'rolling' display." *Beaux-Arts*. Textiles by Hélène Henry and sculpture
by the Martel brothers. Facing page: Foldaway worktop and wire-mesh bottom chair, c. 1930.

FURNITURE

not everywhere. Look at this rosewood table, only the support for the legs is in stainless steel simply because I can't imagine a material better suited to bearing the weight or easier to maintain."[11]

Passionately interested in technical progress, at a very early stage Herbst entered into fruitful collaboration with the industrial sector and he must be regarded as the pioneer of metal furniture in France. The watershed came in 1926. At the Salon d'Automne of that year, he was to present, in partnership with the Electro-Câble company, an office for an engineer made out of sheet metal and tubing, with soundproofed floor and walls, and built-in light fixtures and ventilation. This was something new and created a sensation not only in France but also abroad. The *Manchester Guardian* dated April 5, 1928, headed a column: *A sound-proof room*. Interlocking strips of vulcanized rubber covered floor and walls, soundproofing the reinforced-cement construction, while the ceiling was sectioned into panels that diffused the light and at the same time aerated the space. Not that decoration was banished: broad bands of color swept over floor, walls, and ceiling.

Herbst seems to have applied himself to every basic need, from well-designed offices and comfortable leather armchairs and seats, to sports' equipment. His unusual openness was reiterated in Brussels in 1935 when, in a joint venture with Le Corbusier, Pierre Jeanneret, Charlotte Perriand, and Louis Sognot, he added to an apartment envisioned for "a young man" an exercise room hung with a large painting by Fernand Léger. Now the way was clear, metal furniture featured in every exhibition. At the 1927 Salon d'Automne, Charlotte Perriand exhibited the *Bar sous le Toit,* a determining factor in her entrance to Le Corbusier's. At the 1928 edition, Herbst presented industrial prototypes, a nickel-plated steel dining room with tables and chairs upholstered in Havana brown. The same year, the main event took place at the Salon des Artistes Décorateurs: René Herbst, with Charlotte Perriand and Djo-Bourgeois, joined forces with Gérard Sandoz, Jean Fouquet, and Jean Puiforcat—Herbst

■ Dining room table at M. Peissi's, managing director of OTUA, c. 1930.

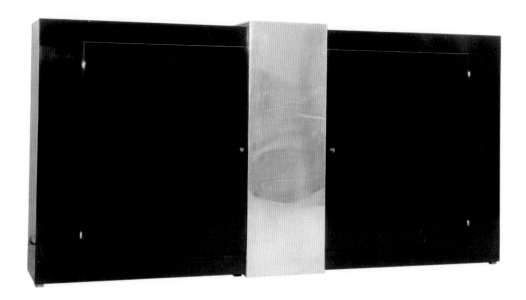

■ Facing page: Two painted-wood and chromium-plated metal side cabinets designed for Henriette Léon's store, 1928 (see store interior p. 52–53).
Above: This display case in painted wood and metal tubing, designed for the bibelot manufacturer Robj, 1927, was used as a bar in the *Smoking room* at the Salon des Artistes Décorateurs, 1928.

showed a smoking room, Perriand a dining room, Djo-Bourgeois a living room, Sandoz and Fouquet jewelry, and Puiforcat goldwork. The exposition, which heralded the setting up of the Union des Artistes Modernes the very next year, sparked off a debate on the modern movement in France. Questions surrounding the advent of metal furnishing were legion at this time: "Must the aesthetics of the bedroom or dining room be the same as that of the automobile or subway carriage?" Jean Gallotti pondered.[12] Though it seemed obvious that "it is the Pavilion of *L'Esprit Nouveau* by Le Corbusier and his team that seems in the process of being realized," nonetheless, Henri Clouzot remarked: "A Salon [is] a laboratory of ideas, [so] it would be imprudent to play the prophet."[13] And yet, as André Boll averred, "standardization is inescapable."[14]

The rapidly growing currency of metal furniture was, however, accompanied by such intellectual confusion that, in June 1932, the Musée Galliera decided to stage an exhibition of metal in art to highlight its long-standing pedigree. The show afforded an insight into the many uses of metal in the past going back to the nineteenth century with lightweight, foldaway pieces such as the canvas and copper campaign tables and chairs used by field marshals in the First Empire—living proof of metal furniture's glorious heritage. The flamboyant 1920s was represented by the wrought iron used by Edgar Brandt, Raymond Subes, and Gilbert Poillerat, and the retrospective was to finish up-to-date with wooden furniture on a chrome- or nickel-plated steel armature by René Herbst, Eugène Printz, and Jacques-Émile Ruhlmann, among others, as well as lighting fixtures, those by Perzel being widely admired. In 1933, the journal *Art et Décoration* initiated an exhibition on metal furniture in its Paris gallery for which Henri Clouzot penned a lavish eulogy on René Herbst whom he had no hesitation in extolling as a leader in his field. "To study René Herbst," as he wrote, "is to recount the history of the avant-garde decorative arts over the last ten years."[15]

■ Metal and wicker fireside chair also to be seen on page 80, in the foreground on the Herbst stand at the UAM Pavilion at the 1937 International Exhibition.

■ Pages 109 to 119: The Aga Khan's private residence at 55 rue Scheffer, Paris. René Herbst completely renovated and revamped the Prince's house, designing and fitting out the entire interior from lights to furniture, 1930–1933. The stained glass on the façade (p. 109) is by Louis Barillet and Jacques Le Chevallier. Pages 110 and 111: Two views of the interior décor. On the ground floor, the rosewood dining room with chairs upholstered in green leather and a glass and chromium-plated steel chandelier (see p. 91); facing, the pure lines of the stairwell.

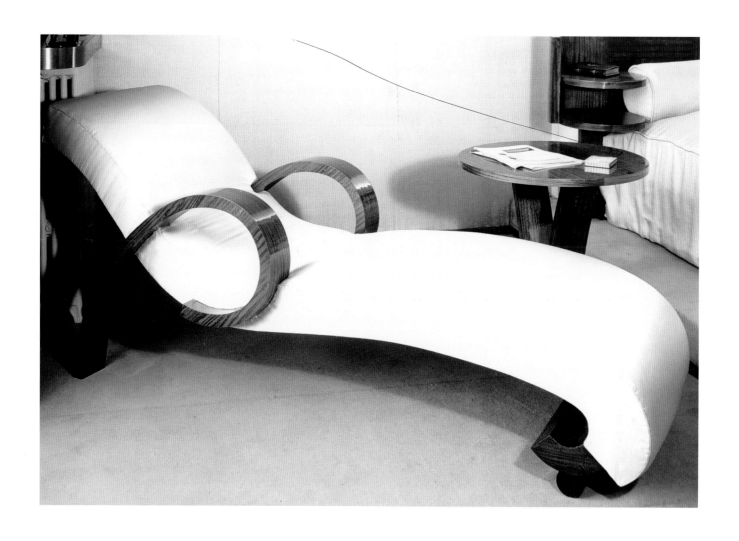

■ Pages 112–113: The Aga Khan's office on the first floor. The stained-glass window alludes to the Prince's keen interest in horses. Above: *Chaise longue* in the Princess's bedroom. Facing page: *Grand salon*. The cornice is lit and the arrangement of the mirror-glass conveys a grandiose impression of space.

■ Pages 116–117: Macassar ebony and satin divan and easychair, glass and chromium-plated steel table.
Above: *Aga Khan dressing-table unit,* small model. Facing page: The bathroom of the Princess Aga Khan.
The Aga Khan dressing-table, large model in mirror glass and painted metal, is visible from the side.

■ Pages 120–121: *Apartment for a young man* designed for the International Exhibition, Brussels, 1935 with Le Corbusier, P. Jeanneret, C. Perriand, Louis Sognot, and Fernand Léger. Here, the fitness room, signed Herbst. On the wall, a mural by Fernand Léger. Above: Bakelite and metal tubing seat, c. 1950.
Facing page: *Director's wood and metal bureau*, with black bakelite chair, c. 1950.

■ Registry office, Boulogne-sur-Seine City Hall (Boulogne-Billancourt, France), varnished mahogany, 1935.

513

SIEGES ACIER R.H

RENE.HERBST   ECHELLE 002 P.M

MASS PRODUCTION AS AN INGREDIENT OF PROGRESS

From the outset, Herbst's aim in researching steel seating had never been to shock or bedazzle the public, but to improve levels of comfort. "In seating design, originality for originality's sake is always a mistake, and for this reason few examples fit the bill," he wrote in 1952.[16] "The chair provides an envelope for the body and, ideally, should be conceived to impart an agreeable sense of repose." Taking his cue from the rows of seats in the arenas of Antiquity, which, worn down by thousands of spectators, afford firm support, he sought an equivalent in advanced materials; the outcome was the famous rubber-strapped chair. "It was for this reason that, some years ago now, I came upon the idea of devising an elastic support which would mold exactly to the form of the body. I attained the ideal solution using rubber [straps] placed almost side by side. Nowadays," he went on, "plastics might make it possible to provide seats and backs perfectly adapted to body shape."

In effect, in the immediate postwar period, ergonomics research pursued energetically on the back of technological developments resulted in the first fiberglass bucket seats that offered unparalleled comfort. The earliest examples were developed as soon 1947 in the United States to designs by Charles Eames and Eero Saarinen for the firms of Knoll and Hermann Miller. Herbst produced a whole range of seats with strapping or stretched with raffia, both armchairs and chaise longues, covered in some cases by fabrics by Hélène Henry, all produced on a large scale.[17] Herbst maintained that mass production offered previously unimaginable possibilities of convenience, in architecture as in furniture and housewares. This "research in improvements in human living standards" in which he wanted a broader public to become involved, was, paradoxically enough, greeted most positively by the upper echelons. Domestic arts *salons* were at this time closely monitored by the intellectual elite. Brunon-Guardia in the journal *L'Intransigeant* wrote:

"Would you like to go to the Salon des Arts Ménagers? I know of elevated minds who gaze in raptures at such domestic improvements. I am acquainted with a poet whose

■ Line drawings for steel chairs designed by René Herbst and published in the 1952 *Formes Utiles* catalog as an illustration for his article on seating and chairs.

MASS PRODUCTION AS AN INGREDIENT OF PROGRESS

joy at the sight of a coolant-based water-heater or a vacuum cleaner knows no bounds."[18] Singularly demanding in terms of design, materials, and methods of manufacture, mass production "will never lend itself to futile decoration; the decorator has no place there,"[19] Herbst explained. "In large volumes, [furniture] must, [like] the car, be impeccably manufactured [and] accessibly priced."[20]

After World War II, the press was to undertake a survey among the pioneers of mass production. When Brunon-Guardia questioned René Gabriel, as well as Yvonne Zervos and René Herbst, all of them replied that only mass production can offer furniture of quality, attractiveness, and practicality at an affordable cost. As Yvonne Zervos—founder of Stylclair, a furniture producer whose contracts in the 1930s had included the launch in France of Marcel Breuer's aluminum furniture—underscored, high volume should not entail low quality but, on the contrary, production that combines perfect detailing with solidity, speed, and low outlay. Turning their backs on competent creators, industrialists for the most part ignored such factors and turned out hybrid pieces in a kind of semi-luxury. As René Herbst himself bitterly reflected:

"When industrialists—except for honorable and moreover rare exceptions—finally take into their heads that one of our models is ripe for mass production, they don't buy it from us—instead, they copy it."[21]

Enlarging on one of his key themes, René Herbst militated in favor of "unique" multi-purpose furniture for offices, living rooms, bedrooms, and kitchens. "Intelligent organization means that the block formed will fit into the smallest apartment . . . In it, man will find everything he needs."[22] He cited one of his most advanced pieces, the meuble *de studio,*[23] mounted at the UAM Pavilion in 1937, which included as he itemized: "Table, bookshelves, wardrobe, filing cabinet, record storage, telephone, typewriter, calculating machine, Dictaphone, wireless, and phonograph." Offering advantages in terms of

■ *Phonograph stand* and *Rosenberg chair,* 1929 (see the suite, p. 92–93 and the drawing, p. 95).

MASS PRODUCTION AS AN INGREDIENT OF PROGRESS

space and comfort, "a single piece in a room adapted to every requirement—this is rational furniture for humankind."

In a talk given to the Amis de l'Art in November 1945, René Herbst outlined his ideas for equipping modern interiors. Adapting living space to changes in contemporary life, he explained, does not mean turning one's back on the past—cars and trams have had no trouble in supplanting horse-drawn carriages and thus transforming the face of the city. The point is to replace what he termed the "bric-à-brac" with spaces that are a pleasure to inhabit. To do so, he continued, one has to throw out all the useless clutter and provide instead novel concepts, pieces of furniture specifically designed for the requirements of modern man. Following his lecture, journalist Sylvain Zegel explained tongue in cheek to readers that at this rate furniture—wardrobes, chests of drawers, sideboards, and the like—which had been their owners' pride and joy from time immemorial, would become obsolescent, ousted by rationally designed *murs utiles*—"functional walls." An empty interior, which in former times had been a sign of poverty, had become the supreme lifestyle luxury. Thus, he concluded provocatively: "In fifty years time, only the poor will own furniture."[24]

■ Collection of metal furniture, c. 1930–1932.

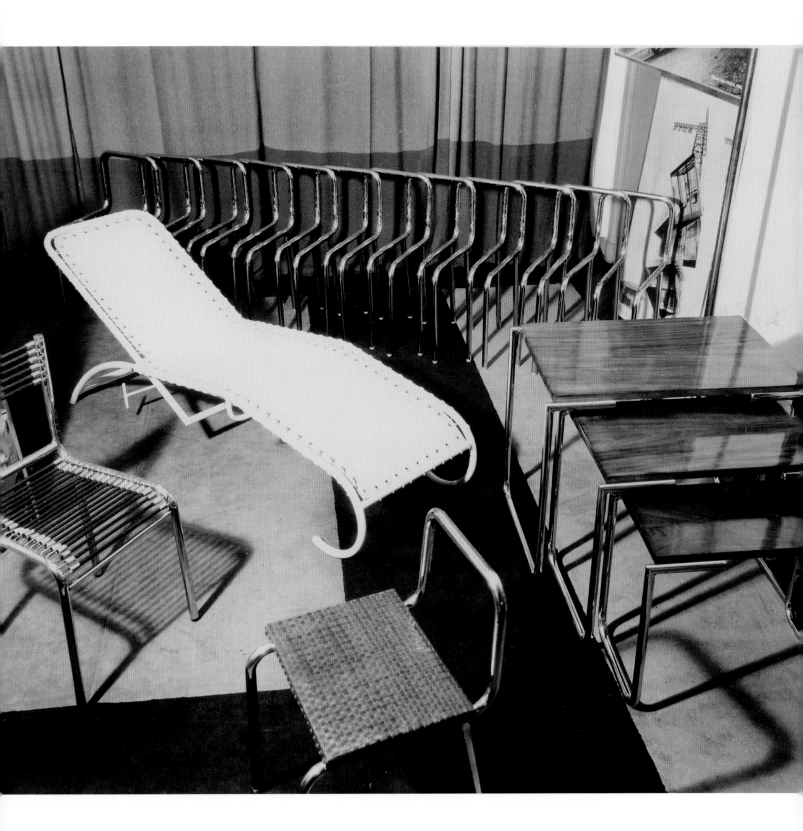

RENÉ HERBST IMPLICATIONS OF A MASS-PRODUCTION CONTEXT

The repercussions of a mass-production context are manifestly both of the aesthetic and the economic orders.

It tends, not to impose outlandish techniques, but, by mechanical means, to render it easier to equip the home. Mass production—an expression that seems to horrify so many—is prevalent in Nature, however. The most beautiful comparison one can make to mass production is perhaps the comparison with all the forms found in Nature. . . .

Mass production offers to all (socially) a potential for comfort unimaginable without it. It is this search for improvements in human living standards that urges us forward to mass production.

Certainly, it's impossible to compare this to earlier times since most then lived in slums. Only mass production allows for the hope of providing a healthy home for every family. . . .

For all that, mass-produced items or articles are not creations intended to make it easier for unscrupulous entrepreneurs to improve their business prospects: for them, large volume is synonymous with low quality when, on the contrary, the quality of manufacture by mechanical means cannot be attained by the hand of the finest craftsman.

One easily becomes emotional about handicraft, the pretty, irregular work by which the artisan imparts, it seems, his heart and soul. For once, one has to show courage and give the lie to such assertions. . . .

A machine, intelligently controlled, is not just less tiring for the workman—the famous robot, ally, and not enemy, of man. It also allows for perfect execution, provided all operations are attentively monitored.

It is an excellent tool, but a tool that can be deflected from its real function. Let us not forget that, if it improves, as I said above, the worker's lot, its impeccable products, rate of production, and cheapness make it a significant factor for the whole manufacturing process.

Mass production will never lend itself to futile decoration and the decorator has no place there. Let us recall that in England, in America, there are many workshops employing draftsmen in both the industrial and building sectors, these artists bring to industry and construction fabulous possibilities as to form, thereby increasing sales.

■ Armature for metal-tubing *chaise longue*. This is the best-known model as it was in the famous palace for the Maharajah of Indore.

RENÉ HERBST IMPLICATIONS OF A MASS-PRODUCTION CONTEXT

France has hardly begun to face up to this situation, but there are extenuating circumstances . . . An over-rich past . . . and, let it be acknowledged, great idleness. It's so easy to revel in the ravishing forms of the past; and, we will also say, there is the unconscionable indifference of those responsible for education.

Because, lest we forget, it is the young who will explain our solutions to problems which, it should be said moreover, have always been wrongly stated.

Mass production covers two doctrines:

Technique (utility)—aesthetics (beauty)

And, recalling Paul Valéry, we say: "utility—beauty—duration." Let us summarize.

The technical doctrine: the machine affords man economical and perfectly manufactured components and utensils.

The esthetic doctrine: if the mass-produced element or object corresponds exactly to its function, if the technique is faultless, if the design of the form is correct, with no exaggeration in one direction or the other, without bluff or fraud, then it will be pure and beautiful. The mass-produced element and article should last; they should be of high quality. That a kitchen table be executed less perfectly than another piece of furniture is unacceptable.

The machine means that an object is of high quality whatever its purpose. The machine is as noble as the hand of the man. Is it not one of the finest creations of his brain and hands?

My visits abroad, particularly to Switzerland and to Scandinavia, have afforded me the opportunity of seeing for myself interiors for workers fitted with standard bookshelves and storage units that allow these men to live a life quite different from ours in their slums.

The day architects grasp the essential role of engineers in housing, mass production will have a significant part to play, and, by use of standard elements, will be able to answer the substantial demand for new dwellings in spite of the complexity of the attendant problems. That standardization necessarily, as is said, obliterates character and style is not a view I share. The old styles were never reproached for using similar elements: moldings, panels, and friezes were employed in series, but assembled in differing ways. . . .

I will conclude by quoting you an extract from Pierre Sonrel. . . . "The development of the utilitarian leads to 'comfort' whereas the pinnacle of the useful is the 'sublime.'"

RENÉ-HERBST,
extract, René Herbst archives

■ Facing page: Drawings for chairs taken from a notebook by René Herbst, *Meubles en métal et en bois (Furniture in metal and in wood).*
Page 137: *Multipurpose furniture* or *Studio unit,* mahogany and sycamore, shown at the UAM Pavilion in 1937, purchased by the Mobilier National in 1938, then placed on deposit at the Musée des Arts Décoratifs, Paris.

00027

FAUTEUIL TUBES, SANDOWS & TISSUS

1928

FAUTEUIL TUBES & TISSUS

PETIT-FAUTEUIL TUBES & TISSUS

1921

00023

00033

1932   FAUTEUIL TUBES SANDOWS & BOIS

RENÉ HERBST MULTIPURPOSE FURNITURE

"Furniture should not resemble intrusive and talkative visitors, but discreet servants who know how not to waylay us with their quaintly eccentric attire or unwarranted eloquence. The only statement to be tolerated on the part of an armchair is an invitation to repose."

Francis Jourdain, Extract from a lecture at the Sorbonne

The unique piece of furniture in a room, adapted to one's needs—this is rational furniture for man. In it, man finds everything he needs. In the room where he works, this includes: his table, his bookshelf, his wardrobe, his filing cabinet, his record storage, the telephone, the typewriter, the calculating machine, the Dictaphone, the wireless, the phonograph.

Intelligent organization means that the block so formed will fit into the smallest apartment. (The piece has been produced and is on show in the Pavilion of the Union des Artistes Modernes at the Exhibition.)

In the living room, it will include: a table (for meals), a cupboard (for dishes), a wine and liqueur cabinet, a special place for folding seats.

In the bedroom, it will include: a place for the linen a closet, the bed.

The multi-purpose unit allows for: 1) practical manufacture 2) impeccable execution 3) advantageous pricing.

This formula is the savior of good quality furniture; indeed, only high quality (good manufacture) can turn the concept into a panacea for our current frenetic lifestyle. Impeccable manufacture: furniture prices can be kept low without a corresponding drop in quality. Indeed, materials and labor alone affect pricing.

The techniques placed at our disposal: plywood, plastics, metals, etc.

Which, when used with appropriate techniques, allow for every kind of product. There is no reason for kitchen furniture to be of low quality; unless the material employed is inferior or the work poorly executed. A very simple furniture design can be produced by machine without the quality being affected. Each material has its own technique; the price is thus a function of this factor and not of the work being executed more or less well. We thus deduce that furniture is not for such and such a class of society, but for different uses; namely: furniture for doing the cooking, for eating on, for working with, for lying down on, etc.

A piece with simple lines, of the same design, executed: in okoume-wood, can cost 1,000 F in Cuba mahogany 2,000 F in stainless steel 3,000 F.

In short, price will be a function of: the materials and techniques used in manufacture (labor, machining, etc.) the use of a material of greater or lesser quality, or poor execution. There exists, thanks to modern technology, first-rate furniture for all.

As for those made in large volumes, they must be, as is currently the case with the car, of impeccable manufacture and accessibly priced.

RENÉ-HERBST,
extract, René Herbst archives

PIONEER
OF A NEW STYLE

LIGHTING

A prominent factor in the modern world, light can transform life: in shop windows, it turns the street into a fairyland. As early as 1921, René Herbst became renowned for his clever use of this remarkable tool in subdued lighting for store display and interiors.[25] He designed a new range of fixtures, including standing floor lamps, table lamps, and suspensions, which, by dint of new technologies, broke with pre-existing forms. For the 1928 Salon d'Automne, he designed a nickel-plated steel ceiling lamp with neon tubes that was to be compared to the shape of a car or airplane[26] as well as to the wings of a soaring gull.[27] Fascination at the time for this new support was such that the Salon d'Automne of 1929 showcased a lighting section, followed, in 1933, by the first Salon de la Lumière. The exhibition, organized the following year by the OCEL[28] on boulevard Haussmann, Paris, presented *artistes du luminaire*—lighting artists. Ceramists and glassmakers such as Daum, Lalique, and Mayodon were integrating lighting into their creations and exhibited shoulder to shoulder with modern designers such as Boris-Lacroix and Max Ingrand, and fabricants like Perzel, Baguès, and Sabino.

The 1937 Exhibition devoted a whole pavilion to light,[29] while Raoul Dufy's *La Fée électricité*, 197 ft. (60 m) long by 33 ft. (10 m) high, created a great stir. The revelation of the 3rd Salon de la Lumière in October 1935 was provided by the UAM's luminescent tubes in which "various gases and vapors generate colored light. Thus, nitrogen, helium, and neon produce yellow, pink, and red, while mercury, cadmium, and sodium vapor send out blue, yellow, and green."[30] Herbst exhibited a luminous panel of colored glass in an arc of a circle shape as a base for a plant stand.[31] With this magical synchronization of sound and color in light, the atmosphere at the exhibition verged on the playful. There was also an illuminated billboard by Jean Carlu, as well as a luminescent globe designed by Robert Mallet-Stevens in collaboration with George Claude. A new profession had been born, modernists proclaimed, that of the lighting engineer, whose place beside the architect and interior designer was soon to become paramount.

■ Cover of a lighting journal, *Lux, La revue de l'éclairage*, no. 3, March 1928; art direction, René Herbst.

LA REVUE DE L'ÉCLAIRAGE

Abonnement : Un An 10 fr.
Étranger, 20 fr., le N° : 1 fr. 25

NUMÉRO 3
MARS 1928

■ Facing page: For the Aga Khan's private residence, rue Scheffer in Paris, Herbst often deployed built-in lighting and mirror-glass, as can be seen here with the luminous cornice in the main drawing room. Page 142: The Princess's bathroom. The chromium-plated metal and glass tubing is at once decorative and functional. Page 143: Chromium-plated steel three-part looking-glass with integrated lighting, presented at the Third Salon de la Lumière, 1935.

■ Pages 144 and 145: *Dining room*, Salon d'Automne, 1928. Chromium-plated, mahogany and Havana furniture, and white and yellow walls. The lighting, realized with André Salomon, features a nickel suspension lamp, "with curves carefully calculated to reflect the light and … redolent of the sweeping, contemporary lines of automobiles and airplanes," *Comœdia*, January 15, 1929.

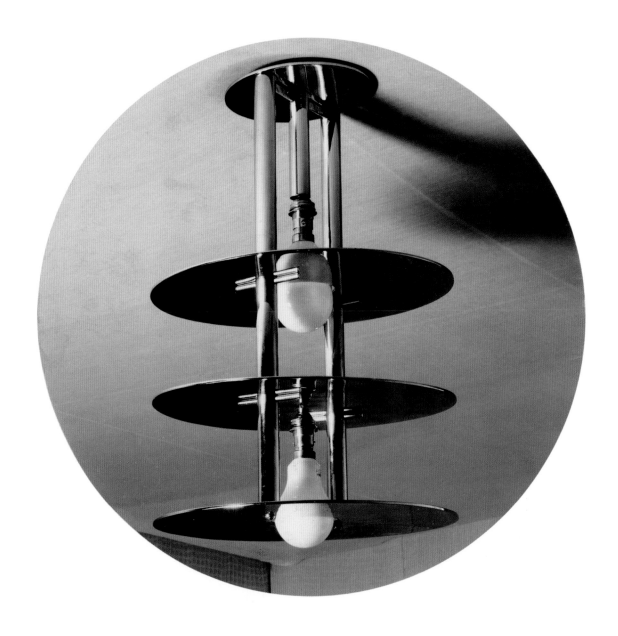

■ Above: Pearl-bulb ceiling-light in nickel-plated steel for an interior in a private house (Depré), 1931.
Facing page: Suspension lamp, 1946.
Page 148: Wall lamps, 1921–1925. Determined to be resolutely modern, from his beginnings René Herbst lavished great care on lighting, and integrated the numerous light fittings he designed into the architecture.

PIONEER
OF A NEW STYLE

STEEL BOAT CABINS

"We live in the century of steel. From the collaboration between engineer and artist works have arisen whose austere beauty, today, can no longer be gainsaid. The astonishing impression of unaffected order, precision, clarity . . . has proved to be the satisfaction of technicians, artists, and public alike. This last understands that steel, in which rails, bridges, ships, engines, cars, armatures, and rolling stock such as locomotives and coaches, are built, is necessary to sustain everyday life."[32]

Herbst proved remarkably accomplished in displaying heavy industrial output when, in 1929 at the International Exhibition at Liège, and again in 1931 at the Colonial Exhibition in Paris, his displays of sheeting and piping as monumental objects confirmed his talent: an increase in scale had done nothing to dampen his imagination. The success of these substantial undertakings was such that, in 1930, Herbst was appointed official collaborator to OTUA (the Technical Office for the Use of Steel), remaining in the post for some thirty years up to the time of the 1961 International Exhibition in Moscow. The position saw him mastermind several events designed to persuade industrialists and the general public as to the technical and aesthetic qualities of steel—in particular, in cabins for a steamer presented at the Grand Palais in 1934 and then at the Musée Galliera in 1936 under the poetic title, *Invitation au voyage*. This was followed by steel school furniture exhibited at the 4th Exposition de l'Habitation in February 1936 and then again at the 1937 International Exhibition.

In 1934, he was to organize studies by teams of architects and industrialists with a view to manufacturing liner cabins in steel incorporating safeguards against fire hazard. Novel technologies developed by the OTUA allowed for removable panels of double-walled sheet steel of which the interstices were plugged with asbestos fiber to improve heat resistance. At less than 55 pounds (25 kg) per square meter, these lightweight steel panels could withstand temperatures above 1,499 °F (815°C) for an hour on one side

■ Page 149: The 2nd Salon de la Lumière at Paris that witnessed the consecration of the profession of the lighting engineer. Opposite page: Cover of the journal *Acier*, no. 1, "Les meubles métalliques," 1930; a publication by the Office Technique pour l'Utilisation de l'Acier (OTUA).

ACIER

LES MEUBLES MÉTALLIQUES

1

1930

N° 1

PUBLIÉ PAR L'OFFICE TECHNIQUE POUR
L'UTILISATION DE L'ACIER
25, RUE DU GÉNÉRAL FOY, PARIS
TÉLÉPHONE : LABORDE 72-13

OTUA

STEEL BOAT CABINS

without the other exceeding 257 °F (125 °C); moreover, the seals absorbed the strain occasioned by the movement of the vessel without undue creaking.[33] The new material demanded a new approach, so the OTUA commissioned René Herbst, as an eminent representative of the modern movement, to head up a competition to impress the advantages of these innovations upon shipbuilding contractors. Against a backdrop of increased maritime transport, the stakes were high. Determined to make the most of this opportunity to combine the efforts of art and industry (an uphill task in France at the time), Herbst turned to his comrades at the UAM. The *concours* was followed by a public exhibition at the Salon d'Automne. Six projects were shown, four of which were executed in conjunction with shipbuildiers: René Herbst in collaboration with the firms of Brès, Calex, Krieg, and Zivi; Robert Mallet-Stevens and the Société Flambo; Pierre Barbe and Ronéo; Marcel Gascoin together with Jean Prouvé's construction business. As for Pierre Chareau and Georges-Henri Pingusson, they showed life-size mock-ups. To this day the whole display remains startlingly modern.

Technical advances came to the fore. Mallet-Stevens's cabin, for instance, could be assembled in sixteen hours by just two workmen. This left the thorny question of the layoffs and unemployment endemic during the economic crises of the 1930s, to which the designer's response was as follows:

"These men readily left off the technique of woodwork to take up steel. The carpenters completed their allotted task perfectly. Some trades are discarded by progress: it is thus necessary to be ready to employ them for other ends. The hackney coachman has become a taxi driver and the joiner abandons timber for work in steel. The architect, the engineer just has to think about it, while the workman has to accept it."[34]

In the main, press coverage was encouraging: "A real revelation, an innovation," exclaimed Léandre Vaillat.[35] While Maximilien Gauthier noted:

■ This basin for a ship cabin free of decorative elements proved a great inspiration for contemporary creators. Pages 154–155: 1st-class steel boat cabin designed by Herbst for the OTUA competition (lighting, A. Salomon, fabrics, H. Henry, trunk, Vuitton), presented at the 1934 Salon d'Automne, and then at the *Invitation au Voyage* show at the Musée Galliera, 1936. Document in color from the journal, *Acier,* July 1935.

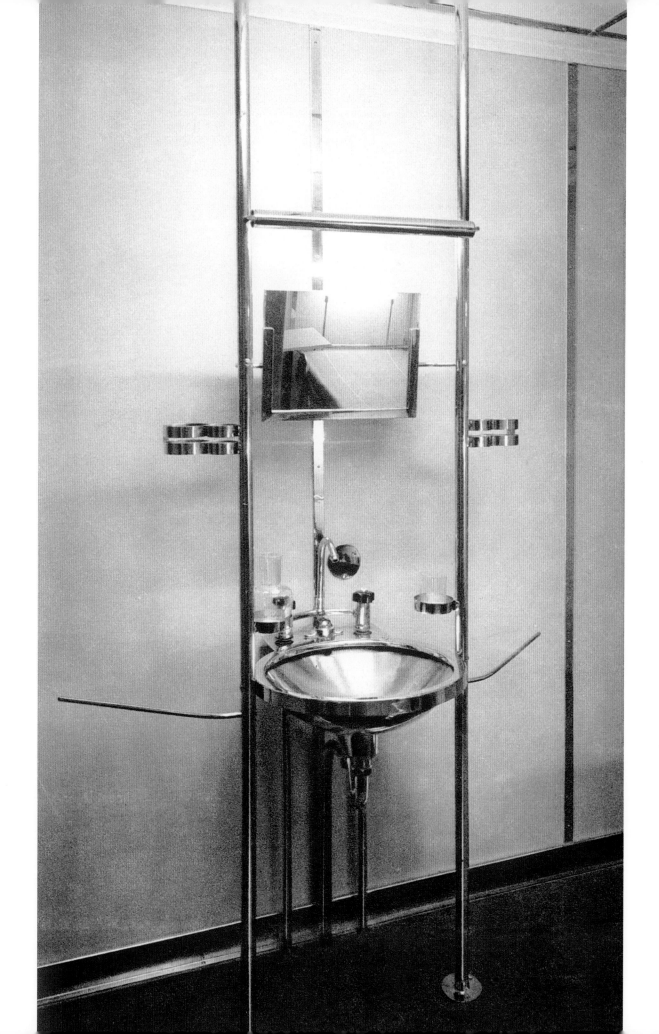

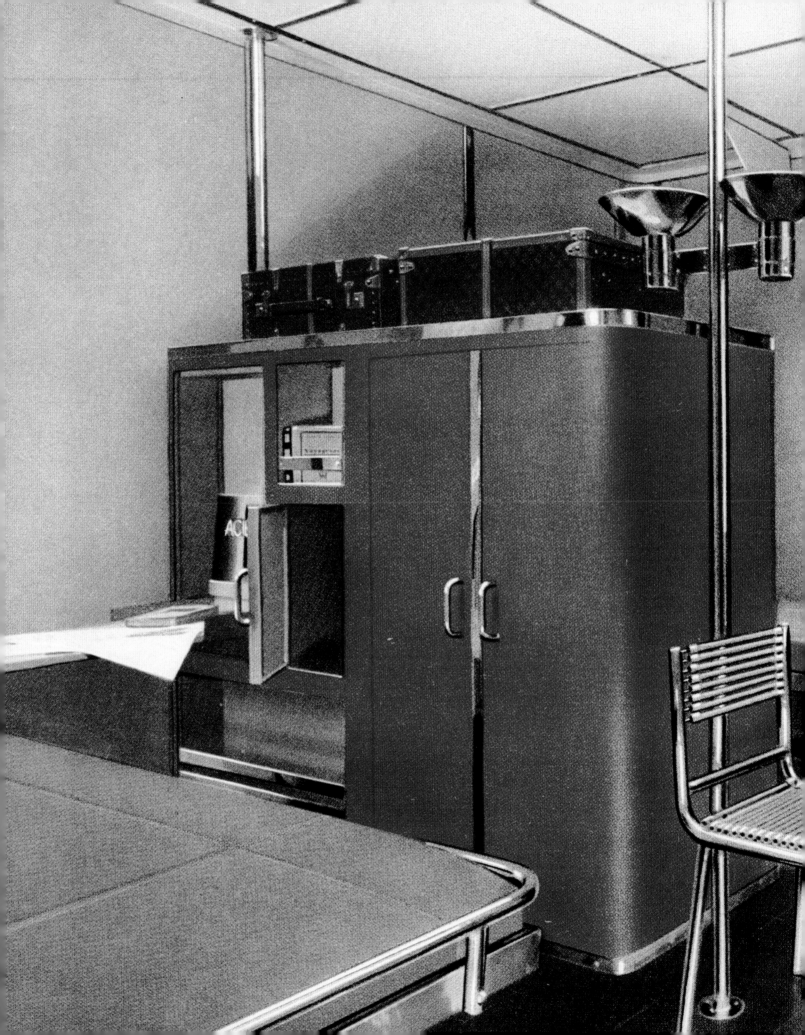

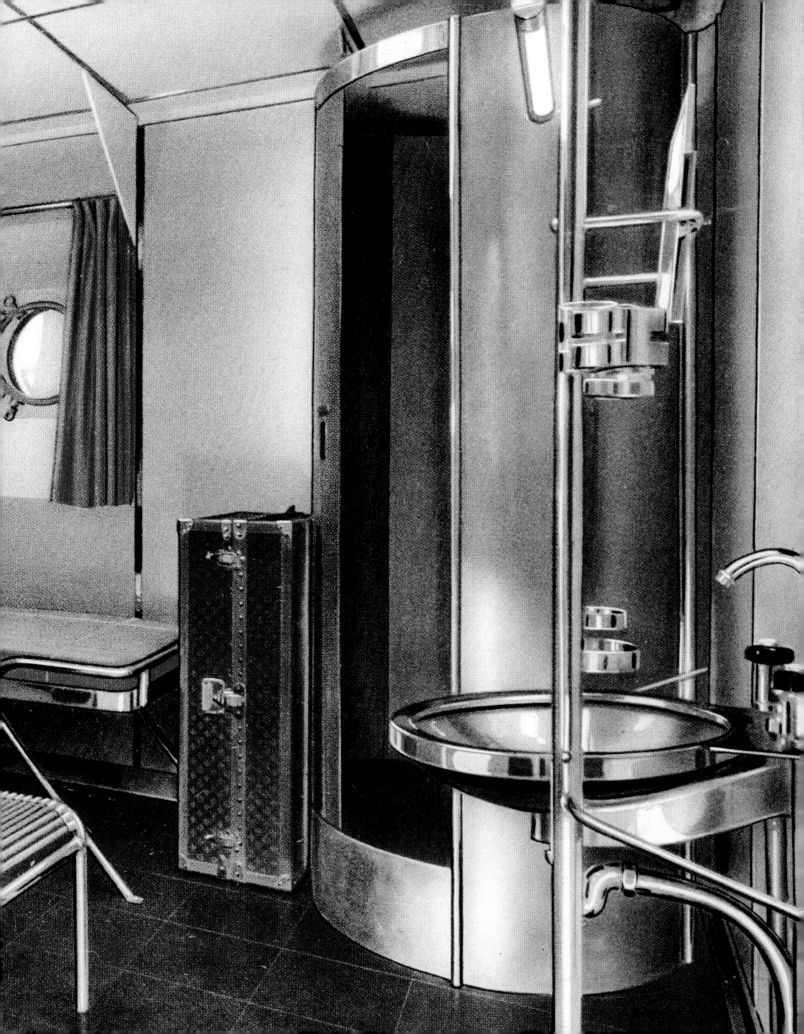

STEEL BOAT CABINS

"Decorative effects are obtained by harmonious relationships between volume and line, by the contrast between polished metal and matt paint. By no means through decorative fantasy."[36]

In spite of the plaudits, the exemplary quality of the plans resulted in no official orders: when the liner *Normandie* was built in 1935, none of the designers taking part in the contest was called upon, as Mallet-Stevens deplored.[37] The incomprehension encountered by modern creatives was only confirmed as the decade progressed. France found it hard to embrace modernity, and, in spite of fulgurating developments in technology, attitudes lagged some way behind.

I. Launched July 14, 1934 at Robert Mallet-Stevens'. **2.** Francis Jourdain, *Les Cahiers Rationalistes*, 1937. **3.** See *Inventory of the Fonds René Herbst*, p. 91–137 of present work. **4.** *Paris Midi*, 1923. **5.** 2nd UAM exhibition, May 1931. **6.** 3rd UAM exhibition, March 1932. **7.** The exhibition *Metals in Art*, June 1932. **8.** 4th UAM exhibition, 1933. **9.** Salon d'Automne, 1933. **10.** *French Decorative Art*, Galerie Bernheim-Jeune, 1934. **11.** René Herbst correspondence, *Le Figaro Illustré* (August 31, 1931), René Herbst Archives. **12.** Jean Gallotti. *Revue Hebdomadaire* (July 1928). **13.** Henri Clouzot. *L'Opinion* (December 11, 1926). **14.** André Boll, *Le Temps*. **15.** *L'Industriel Savoisien*, April 1933. **16.** *Le Siège*, René Herbst Archives. Published in the *Formes Utiles* catalog, 1952. **17.** See illustrations of side views of seats from 1926–1950, pp. 122, 126, 129, 131, 133, 135 of the present work. **18.** G. Brunon-Guardia, *L'Intransigeant* (February 3, 1935). **19.** *Implications of a mass-production environment*, René Herbst Archives, p. 132–135 of the present work. **20.** *Multipurpose furniture*, René Herbst Archives, p. 136–137 of the present work. **21.** G. Brunon-Guardia, interview with René Herbst in *La Liberté* (October 9, 1937). **22.** *Multi-purpose furniture*, p. 136–137. **23.** The piece is now in the collections of the Musée des Arts Décoratifs, on deposit at the Mobilier National. **24.** Sylvain Zegel, article collected by René Herbst, no title or date reference. **25.** The ceiling lights in the Aga Khan residence in particular. **26.** *Comœdia* (January 15, 1929). **27.** *La Liberté*, n. d. **28.** OCEL: Office Central Électrique. **29.** Robert Mallet-Stevens and Georges-Henri Pingusson, architects, and André Salomon, engineer. **30.** Gaspard Brunet, *L'Industrie laitière* (November 1935). **31.** Reproduced in *Art et Décoration* (1935): p. 417. **32.** *Nord Industriel* (November 1, 1930). **33.** Emmanuel de Thubert, "L'acier sur la mer," *La Construction moderne* (January 13, 1935): p. 351. **34.** Quoted by Maximilien Gauthier, *Les Nouvelles Littéraires* (November 1934). **35.** *Le Temps* (November 7, 1934). **36.** *Les Nouvelles Littéraires* (November 1934). **37.** *L'Architecture d'Aujourd'hui* (August 1935).

■ Steel *Basin-cum-shower*. Photomontage by René Herbst.

THE FOUNDATION OF THE UAM

Rene Herbst had a talent for groups. This had been evident as early as 1923 when he joined Francis Jourdain, Robert Mallet-Stevens, and Pierre Chareau in an exhibition at the urban art section recently set up at the Salon d'Automne. It marked the onset of some long-standing friendships, as well as of a heartfelt respect for Jourdain whom he regarded as the most significant figure of his generation. It was also the beginning of a career marked by unflagging activism. This central core was to expand. In June 1929, the UAM was created, followed, after the hiatus of the war years, by the Formes Utiles association, whose principal aim was to increase public awareness.

The 1920s witnessed a burgeoning interest in collective exhibitions in the applied arts, and little by little, splinter groups appeared. In 1926, Pierre Chareau, Jean Puiforcat, Raymond Templier, and Pierre Legrain, young artist-decorators who reckoned themselves inadequately represented at the 1925 Exhibition in what they styled the "hubbub" of the Grand Palais, organized an exposition of their own at the Barbazanges gallery[38] that abandoned the practice of tutelage under an authoritarian coordinator for a collective based on shared affinities. René Herbst, Charlotte Perriand, and Djo-Bourgeois had laid the bases for the Union des Artistes Modernes when, in 1928, they exhibited together at the Salon des Artistes Décorateurs in an autonomous body, which, in an inclusive spirit, embraced goldsmiths and jewelers such as Jean Puiforcat, Jean Fouquet, and Gérard Sandoz. Taking as their emblem a bit-brace that they erected in the vestibule,[39] they did not go unnoticed. "Herbst, Djo-Bourgeois, Perriand are part of an avant-garde movement that surely owes very little to their elders. . . . And in their glorious wake, they have brought with them many other artists," Waldemar George enthusiastically recorded.[40] Emboldened by the success of a first experiment that saw them feted for the new ideas it embodied, the group would have liked to repeat it, but they ran up against a refusal on the part of the Société des Artistes Décorateurs.

■ Facing page: Cover to the catalog for the 1st exhibition of the UAM at the Musée des Arts Décoratifs, 1930. The UAM logo was created by Pierre Legrain. Pages 160–161: *Music room,* 1st exhibition of the UAM, display on a sloping black floor, including a "Herbst model" Pleyel piano in mahogany and nickel-plated metal, a green baize bridge table and green stretched rubber bottom chairs. Textiles by Hélène Henry.

PREMIERE EXPOSITION DE L'UNION DES ARTISTES MODERNES

MUSÉE DES ARTS DÉCORATIFS PAVILLON DE MARSAN
II JUIN - 14 JUILLET 1930

PIONEER
OF A NEW STYLE

THE FOUNDATION OF THE UAM

Their frustration was redoubled by the fact that the profession's commercial and industrial sectors were gaining the upper hand over creativity, especially in the wake of the triumph at the 1925 Exhibition of the department stores' generic workshops. This then was the reason behind the split at the heart of the Société des Artistes Décorateurs: in June 1929, twenty-five of its members sensationally resigned and announced the creation of the Union des Artistes Modernes,[41] an association headed not by a president but by a steering committee. The first event staged by this new society took place at the Musée des Arts Décoratifs in June 1930 and brought together an eclectic group of practitioners from every artistic discipline bound by a common faith in a future-orientated modern art. The exhibition, curated by Mallet-Stevens with the assistance of specialist lighting engineer André Salomon, presented furniture (by Francis Jourdain, René Herbst, Jean Prouvé, Charlotte Perriand in collaboration with Le Corbusier and Pierre Jeanneret, Eileen Gray, Pierre Barbe, Louis Sognot, and Charlotte Alix), fabrics (Hélène Henry), lighting (Jean Dourgnon, Jacques Le Chevallier), posters (Jean Carlu, Paul Colin), jewelry (Jean Fouquet, Gérard Sandoz, Raymond Templier, and Etienne Cournault), tableware (Jean Puiforcat), articles in ivory (Georges Bastard), stained glass (Louis Barillet), sculpture (Jan and Joel Martel, Joseph Csaky, and Gustave Miklos), and photography (Man Ray). The UAM also showed bookbinding by the lamented Pierre Legrain in homage to one of its founder members and the originator of its insignia. Foreign, including German and Dutch, designers were also invited, Gerrit Rietveld among them.

This self-governing group of artists of diverse outlook linked by shared aspirations constituted an innovative step: imperceptibly, the modern spirit was percolating through to at least most of the Salons. If the UAM had dissented from the Salon des Artistes Décorateurs owing to what was deemed unacceptable modernism, in that same year of 1930, the Décorateurs invited the Werkbund from Germany, similar in tendency to the UAM.

■ Facing page: The UAM's manifesto, *Pour l'art moderne, cadre de la vie contemporaine,* drawn up with the collaboration of Louis Chéronnet. The Press was invited to a launch soirée at Robert Mallet-Stevens' house on July 14, 1934. Pages 164–165: *Small drawing room,* Salon d'Automne, 1929. The ceiling light surprised some visitors: the central element of the composition was a plain pearl light bulb only partially concealed by a metal disk.

POUR

L'ART MODERNE

CADRE DE LA VIE CONTEMPORAINE

THE FOUNDATION OF THE UAM

It took a brief lapse of time for the reaction to set in, and it was 1931 or 1932 before detractors found their voice. Perusing the press cuttings made by Herbst plunges us back into that time; there were commentators who maintained they were faced by a new academism, a kind of "superstition of form,"[42] while others essayed a more moderate tone: "These artists of the UAM have the mentality of a decorator in 1900. . . . Simply put, the iris, mistletoe, and sunflower have been replaced by nuts and bolts."

The debate revolved around whether ornament was still relevant. But, they enquired, what does the word "ornament" actually mean? Pierre du Colombier stressed the fact that "to apply the word ornament solely to what is added is too narrow a meaning. There are ornamental ways of treating a form." It was an argument backed by those who had it that the UAM's members were "indulging in '*machinerie*' just as certain *décorateurs* of the eighteenth century indulged in '*chinoiserie*' and '*turquerie*.'"[43] The critique addressed not only what was seen as austerity ("True decorative Quakerism. A miserable art"[44]) but also the choice of materials: "The plastic potential of metal and that of glass is too limited, while the starkness of some of the furniture results in the negation of all individuality, even of art itself."[45] Another ploy was to detect an alien influence: "[It marks] the triumph of a Protestant aesthetic brought in from Holland and Germany." To counter such misgivings—uttered against a background of an economic crisis that had grown particularly acute in the luxury goods sector—on July 14, 1934 the members of the UAM organized at Mallet-Stevens's an "express" exhibition—it lasted two hours—at which they launched a manifesto, *Pour l'art moderne*.[46] In the preamble they declare: "We believe that art has to exist in a state of permanent revolution," before embarking on a point by point refutation of the attacks made on them—on the pros and cons of ornament, on the "horrors" of sparseness, on the *style paquebot*, on society and art, on art in the economic slump—peppering this discussion with a wealth of references to the world's artistic heritage.

■ Facing page: The UAM Exhibition at the Musée des Arts Décoratifs, 1932. Jean Carlu's poster for disarmament in the background created a scandal: considered subversive, it was removed for the inauguration by the Minister of Fine Arts. It was reinstated following complaints from UAM.
Pages 168–169: UAM Exhibition, front hall, June 1, 1933, with rubber-strap chairs and a nest of metal tables.

**PIONEER
OF A NEW STYLE**

With an argument shored up by a list of miscellaneous examples from every conceivable period, they proclaimed loud and clear:

"Adaptation to progress, which is a law of life, has never detracted from the quality of artistic endeavor. . . . We favor balance, logic, and purity. In housing, we prefer light to shade, merry hues to drab colors. . . . We think we can esthetically combine practical convenience with psychological mood, i.e. with one that better expresses the personality of its occupant. We dream of vast, salubrious, well-ventilated cities, with cheerful green spaces. . . . In addition to the old duet of wood and stone, which we have never neglected, we have also attempted to assemble a quartet featuring cement, glass, metal, and electricity, a harmonious quartet whose principles we have attempted to determine and whose chords we have worked to uncover. Like others before us, we have had recourse to every artistic métier without exception . . . , we have appealed for aid from the decorative sculptor, we have never spurned collaboration with painters, we have breathed new life into stained glass, we have neglected neither humble heating nor lofty lighting. Lastly, we have even descended into the street, so that advertising billboards too can enjoy their share of beauty."

Unsettled, critics wondered earnestly whether this tendency would stay the course. Admittedly, Salons served as laboratories where the interiors of tomorrow could be seen today,[47] but was all this upheaval a brief interlude or a seachange?

Louis Vauxcelles demanded to know whether the "'theoretical intoxication'" that grips both the Werkbund and the French prophets of *L'Esprit Nouveau*, "whether all this systematization, this standardization, [was] a passing fad or a style? These dentist, these sanatorium chairs, this Puritanism, the architectonic bareness of this 'machine for living'—are these beginners', idlers' efforts—or a truly new mode of living?"[48] Guillaume Janneau, administrator at the State-owned Mobilier National, was puzzled.

■ Pages 170–171: UAM Exhibition at the Galerie de la Renaissance, 1933. René Herbst presents the satin canapé for the Princess Aga Khan. Facing page: School furniture at the Salon d'Automne, exhibit by UAM, 1936. Pages 174–175: Bird's-eye view showing the 1937 International Exhibition of Arts and Techniques in which can be seen the German Pavilion at the foot of the Trocadéro and the Seine at the Iéna Bridge.

THE FOUNDATION OF THE UAM

"The problem facing contemporary decorative art is precisely this: is it a laboratory creation or does it possess the characteristics of a style?"[49]

To those he dubbed makers of furniture that resembled cycle handlebars, André Lhote meanwhile declared simply: "These artists write on sand."[50] The most virulent reaction came from Waldemar George: "Modern art is one hundred percent sick. In the eyes of the young, Le Corbusier . . . is no more than a fossilized architect. . . . The most intransigent revolutionaries defend tradition, national handiwork, and an art bearing the stamp of the homeland. . . . We lament the loss of neither *faux* Henri II, nor *faux* Directoire, nor even the *faux rustique*. Is this though sufficient reason for declaring the gracious Mme. Charlotte Perriand's rudimentary sitting machines or M. René Herbst's line drawings in agreement with the spirit of the French and Cartesian tradition?"[51] A surprising volte-face indeed coming from someone who had loudly applauded their audacity in 1928.

Indeed, the 1930s were to witness a U-turn in opinion that mirrored the drastic socioeconomic situation: the Utopian era was well and truly at an end.

38. From April 1 to 15, 1926, information provided by the "Chronique des Arts" of the journal *L'Art Vivant* (1926). **39.** Léandre Vaillat, *Le Temps* (June 12, 1928). **40.** Waldemar George, *Le Journal de l'Ameublement* (June 1928). **41.** The general meeting establishing the UAM was held on May 29, 1929 at Hélène Henry's, quai des Grands-Augustins. The steering committee comprised Francis Jourdain, Robert Mallet-Stevens, Hélène Henry, and René Herbst, with Raymond Templier acting as secretary. Some twenty-three in number, its active membership included Sonia Delaunay, Eileen Gray, Charlotte Perriand, Pierre Barbe, Louis Barillet, Jean Burkhalter, Joseph Csaky, Jean Fouquet, Robert Lallemant, Jacques Le Chevallier, Le Corbusier, Pierre Jeanneret, Pierre Legrain, Pablo Manes, Gustave Miklos, Jean Prouvé, Jean Puiforcat, Gérard Sandoz, and André Salomon. **42.** *Le Crapouillot* (March 1932). **43.** François Fosca, *Je suis partout* (May 20, 1931). **44.** Eugène Marsan, *Le Figaro*, n. d. **45.** *Beaux-Arts* (February 25, 1932). **46.** *Pour l'art moderne, cadre de la vie contemporaine*, manifesto drafted with the literary collaboration of Louis Chéronnet. **47.** Léandre Vaillat, *Le Temps* (June 12, 1928). **48.** *L'Excelsior* (February 11, 1932). **49.** *L'Exportateur français* (October 13, 1932). **50.** *Beaux-Arts* (February 28, 1932). **51.** *La Revue Mondiale* (December 10, 1935).

■ Facing page: Printing and graphic arts at the 1937 UAM Exhibition. The highly didactic exhibit featured manufacturing processes and highlighted fonts by Peignot. Pages 178–179: *Advertising with words, advertising with pictures*, 1937 Exhibition. A neon strip light gives added impact to a wall dealing with the Press.

FOR A HUMANE
ARCHITECTURE

4

formes utiles

sélection de l'Union des Artistes Modernes

l'équipement sanitaire
le siège

USEFUL FORMS

"The current social situation is due primarily to life in the slums. When all are able to live in an environment in keeping with human existence, immense strides will have been taken towards a better life." RENÉ HERBST

Returning to the fray shortly after the War in the guise of the Club Mallet-Stevens, the Union des Artistes Modernes chaired by Rene Herbst[1] issued a proclamation entitled *Manifeste 1949*. Recalling its determination to labor for an "art of our time [from] town planning to the lowliest everyday article,"[2] the UAM stressed the importance of the selection of household goods and the rationalization of home appliances. These ideas were to materialize in the exhibition "Useful Forms, Objects of Our Time," organized at the Musée des Arts Décoratifs in December 1949.[3] The scope of the exhibition embraced everyday consumer articles produced by craftsmen or industrials which, though commonplace, were selected for their effectiveness. Thus the group rekindled Francis Jourdain's 1936 plans[4] for a "bazaar" featuring "anonymous intelligent objects, valiant, honest objects, beautiful because they are intelligent, which please the eye because they please the mind."[5] Continuing the endeavors of their predecessors at the time of Art Nouveau to get "useful art" recognized as a proper art, they exhibited these contemporary objects adjacent to objets d'art which had already acquired masterpiece status. Their slogan, "forms are useful (and beautiful) when they satisfy the requirements of their materials and the aspirations of the mind," paralleled the motto the Musée des Arts Décoratifs had adopted at its foundation—"the beautiful in the useful."[6] This eminently laudable aim had nevertheless proved difficult to attain since few undertook to fulfill the appeal's specific criteria.[7] The reasons for the scarcity of "modest, inexpensive articles" noted at the debut selection derived essentially, as it had at the end of the nineteenth century, from shortcomings in education, among the public as well as among creators.

■ Page 181: Catalog of the exhibition *Formes Utiles,* Musée des Arts Décoratifs, 1952, by Jacques Nathan.
Opposite page: Exhibition *Formes Utiles,* Salon des Arts ménagers, Grand Palais, 1959.

■ Exhibition *Formes Utiles,* Musée des Arts Décoratifs, 1949 with children's school furniture. The photo on page 185 was modified by René Herbst.

40 années de métier
40 photographies

René Herbst

Paris 1949

In adumbrating a theory of the "useful forms" concept,[8] André Hermant proposed to shift the criteria from an aesthetic basis to an ethical one. Thus, Hermant suggested, one might speak of the "truth of a chair," "the straightforwardness of a coffeemaker," or "the hypocrisy of a façade." Following logical progression, he contended that something produced by humankind is "true" when it conveys a harmonious balance between function, structure, and form. Addressing the issue of the assembly line, as a corollary of the industrially produced object Hermant took the example of plants in Nature, noting that they have the same function, are made from the same materials, and yet are possessed of extraordinary variety of form.[9]

Twenty years after its first manifestation, the UAM was to experience a new lease on life with, in the ambit of the Salon des Arts Ménagers, yearly showcases for basic houseware: furniture and table settings, as well as hardware, electrical and medical appliances, cladding materials, etc. In reply in 1964 to Pascal Renous[10] concerning the transformation of the UAM into "Formes Utiles," René Herbst explained that it had proved impossible to confine its remit to the strictly artistic field: the contribution of industry had become indispensable. "At bottom, what we don't want is to be considered as 'aestheticians.'" He went on to reiterate their objective of defending a modern art that would serve as a backdrop to life in the contemporary world: it was and is a question of taking account of the exigencies of function and material to create "forms corresponding to a real need," and not for amusement.

■ "40 years in the trade, 40 photographs," cover for a spiral-bound notebook made by René Herbst in 1949.

Inside the right image:

1956

formes utiles

Union des Artistes
Modernes
1956
septième exposition
Formes Utiles

Trois sections :
La table des repas.
Le service de table.
Le couvert de table.

■Pages 188, 189, 190, and 191: A number of catalog covers for *Formes Utiles*, published for
the annual exhibitions organized at the Grand Palais by the Salon des Arts Ménagers. Graphics
by Jean Lhuer in 1956 (p. 188) and by Pierre Faucheux in 1953 (p. 189) and in 1954 (p.190–191).

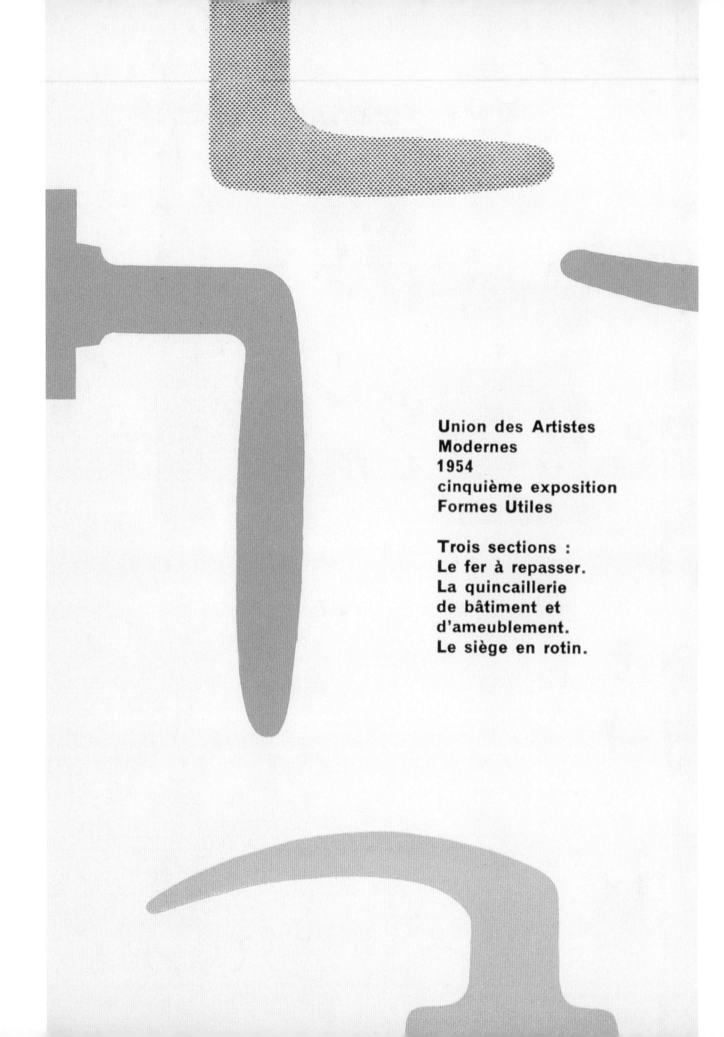

Union des Artistes
Modernes
1954
cinquième exposition
Formes Utiles

Trois sections :
Le fer à repasser.
La quincaillerie
de bâtiment et
d'ameublement.
Le siège en rotin.

FORMES UTILES

1 9 5 4

RENÉ HERBST INTERIOR DECORATION AND ITS TECHNIQUES

With each passing day it becomes increasingly evident that simplicity is not synonymous with impoverishment and that a civilized person, if he has other needs, other requirements, than the savage, faces other difficulties too. He is more sensitive to beauty of proportion, of the relationship between surfaces, volumes, and lines, and more easily offended by a superficial decoration which beguiles the eye alone, which addresses only the animal in him. One has, one has above all, to speak to the mind. This, to my way of thinking, is the problem that today confronts all those concerned with building housing for modern man.

We have to strive to satisfy the spirit as we strive to satisfy the eye. It has become commonplace to repeat that an architectural form is beautiful only when determined by function, but we have now to concede that it satisfies our eye precisely because it satisfied our mind beforehand—by which I mean the mind's need for logic, for order, for clarity.

We can no longer live amid bric-à-brac. We should clear out—de-furnish.

We find ourselves, furthermore, before an obligation arising from a sort of conflict between the development of civilization and economic evolution; our need for comfort has grown but the space we have at our disposal has decreased. We no longer possess the right, nor the means, to waste space for purely decorative effects. Luxurious great halls already belong to the past; the installation of small rooms (that is, those best adapted to an increasing number of needs in progressively limited surfaces)—this is the specifically modern problem.

We can no longer put off tackling this: the solution—incompatible with the "beautiful disorder" of the artist—lies in severe purification, rigorous and imperative in character, which will, ultimately, be wholly beneficial to art.

. . . A negative measure, then? Yes, but an infinitely reasonable one, which, were it applied, would help to overcome outdated notions of luxury and draw a line separating the moneyed aristocracy from an aristocracy of taste. Any parvenu can turn his interior into a museum or junk store. But only a man of sensitivity knows that money has no direct effect on beauty; only he knows the exigencies, not of his outer life alone, but of his inner life as well. His luxury will consist in being immersed in forms adapted to his material needs whose purity satisfies his spiritual needs—that is, his reason.

Reason can find no content in disorder: the imagination alone is not enough to gratify the intelligence. The sight of a cheap plate does not unsettle one's reason; it is, however, shocked and outraged by a dish by Bernard Palissy. A piece of furniture by Gallé is a mistake, or a folly rather: the artist who makes an armchair so as to interpret a line of Baudelaire just creates a muddle.

Modern man awaits a dwelling combining the most practical, most concrete kind of comfort with the least apparent, most abstract kind of luxury.

Reduced to its bare essentials, such an environment verges on a kind of anonymity that prevents the personality of its creator (engineer, even artist) becoming a burdensome presence for an occupant who senses its art in a near unconscious manner.

I would like, as I mentioned a few moments ago, to draw your attention to the total ignorance of the masses with respect to interior architecture. . . .

Machines, our detractors say, have killed inner life. And why? Because we want furniture doors to operate in new ways, windows to slide silently, furniture to be made in steel because it is easier to produce in large quantities and at low price? Because we want chairs to be more comfortable by the incorporation of new, more flexible springs, and lighter thanks to tubular steel frames, etc.?

The machine is for us, for people of modest tastes, something necessary. But why shy away from its qualities? Why does a man of talent, like M. Paul Iribe, launch diatribes that sow confusion in every mind?

I concede: we'll take the machine—and I'll leave him those precious masterpieces that have no place in our interiors. Such masterpieces exist to instruct and it is always with joy that we walk through the museums that are their final resting place.

M. Iribe has not shrunk from publishing a booklet attacking the modern idiom in art in which he announces to all and sundry: "Just look what modern art would be like were I entrusted with creating furniture, jewelry, cars, houses." He is an eclectic man, we all knew him before the war, we could all gauge his great talent for ourselves. But since then, only one thing counts, that's the work, and, up to now, he has done nothing but write. What has happened to M. Iribe happens to the vast majority. It is blind. It seems bereft of sensitivity. Why do they want the French brand alone to be known for futile trinkets and *grand luxe?* . . .

A man exhausted after work needs air, psychological repose: the family [needs] to rest visually: Nature. We have thus to provide him with a framework worthy of his family; broad bay windows to let in the air and allow him to gaze outside. He will also need seating on which his resting body leaves the mind in quietude.

Let us not forget that the average mortality rate over the whole of France is as high as 18%. In garden cities, it falls to 4.9%. This is a rebuff we might address to all our deprecators: out of a hundred or so children living in a healthy house, four die; while in the slums, that figure is multiplied fivefold.

The problem for us today can be simply stated. The house is a cell that has to shelter a family. It is, if you like, a cube. The cube, for some, is synonymous with death. While for us it is synonymous with health.

RENÉ HERBST INTERIOR DECORATION AND ITS TECHNIQUES

An interior must be adapted to family needs. A mother who runs herself into the ground for her loved ones looks for minimum exertion for maximum benefit. Simple furniture suited to its function. Drawers on quiet roller tracks (roller bearings are invisible and will not spoil the appearance of the piece in any way).

Fitted cupboards with swivel or sliding doors. *This* is what Interior Architecture is. The whole organization forms a unit with the building and has nothing to do with pure decoration. What is its aim? Health for one's family avoiding contamination. No more moldings or reliefs likely to trap dust. Air, color, and gaiety.

. . .There should be no decoration at all. It's a frame and nothing else. Farewell to all the hideous accessories. Do not undermine the values of Nature—she has always known best.

RENÉ-HERBST,
Lecture at the CPDT,
Extracts, May 4th, 1932

■ Above: Mahogany and steel phonograph center.
Facing page: Table and chairs, 3rd UAM Exhibition, Musée des Arts Décoratifs, 1932.

RENÉ HERBST ORGANIZING THE HOME

The kitchen. Principle: everything should be tidied away. Immediately, Mesdames, I can see you smile. You are saying to yourselves: "Very practical, a kitchen in which you can't see anything. If I need a saucepan, I have to open a cupboard; if I need a bottle, I have to open another cupboard."

In the kitchen, there are two wall cupboards. One just for those things you need to cook food—bottles, utensils, etc. You go into the kitchen to prepare a meal: you open the two cupboards and instantly you have everything you require to set to work.

Your kitchen is small; it doesn't need to be big because we have no wish for the kitchen to be somewhere to sit and take meals in. You'll find it far easier to move around a small kitchen when the cupboards are correctly situated with respect to your needs.

To one side, you have your stove, a board specially for preparing food, and a sink with two taps above with hot and cold water. The cold water is equipped with a purifier. Everything should be close at hand to reduce movement and fatigue to a minimum.

Do not forget that a kitchen it is a laboratory. I can see you smiling again: "A few moments ago, it was a clinic and now it's a laboratory." The definition is not mine; it is a physician's, M. de Pommiami.

Permit me to cite this sentence from the foreword to his book: "Cooking a foodstuff means modifying it by heat. In modifying it, one alters its constitution and its constitution is its chemistry." The use of fire is physics. Remind yourselves that the kitchen is the anteroom of happiness. Allow me, Mesdames, to open its doors to you.

The walls of your kitchen must be kept healthy; gloss-painted if possible, or else lined with white tiles. It is up to the decorator to find that nuance that tempers the chilliness of white paint. One could have a bright-colored stripe to liven it up and the bay window airing it will allow unexpected effects, thanks to the ever-changing sky.

At night, a kitchen must be lit by a high-output central light with diffuser. A kitchen should be extremely well illuminated, let us not forget, and light implies cleanliness.

Let us move on to the main family room. A communal room, in which the family lives. The English possess a splendid word for this room: "Living room." In French the only word is *pièce commune*—"communal, common room,"—which I acknowledge is not particularly beautiful. It is in this communal room that meals are taken.

It is where the family meets up. Here, the architect needs to exploit every possibility the layout of the other rooms permits. If there's a free corner, he could envisage a cupboard-cum-dresser. He might fit something out in wood so as to provide a bookshelf or chair. To one side, an entirely open wall gives on a terrace. If we are in a city, install a hanging garden; if in the countryside, there's the view over Nature.

We don't want man to feel isolated in his house, as if in a cage. The furniture of the communal room has to be kept simple. Wood offers a cheery note. Let us avoid sharp corners and round off anything likely to injury our children. And what is more pleasant than to pass one's hand over something smooth, without edges? (We've come a long way from the aggressive cube.)

The floor should be washable: linoleum, rubber, or cork. If you reside in an entire house, you might have paving or a plastic that is easy to lay. In the cozier parts of the room, throw down a rug. A thick-pile wool rug perhaps, made [with the means at one's disposal].

It must be simple, almost plain. A dash of color is sufficient. Do not forget that wanting to imitate Nature is a mistake. It is too beautiful and we are too clumsy.

Lighting might be installed in two stages: a main light that should flood [the room] with light, but not dazzle. And then portable lamps at the disposal of individual readers. Your walls should always be pale-colored.

Do not forget that color absorption is a significant factor in lighting. If you employ white, you will obtain 80% of the output, light pink 65%, yellow 70%, with dark blue we immediately drop to 25%, light gray 55%, dark gray 20%, and dark green 30%.

Over certain stretches of the wall, one could try fabric. It does not need to portray a scene. It should be virtually plain; texture alone should give it life. You are still being told that modern decorators can only use plain things. How wrong that is! I invite you all to visit the workshop belonging to a young woman who supplies us all, Mme. Hélène Henry.

She is an artist who is not satisfied with simply providing fabric for covering walls and furniture; she strives, through a mixture of points, to bring out all qualities of the materials she employs. And don't go thinking that all her textiles are luxury textiles. They are made for everyone and suit any kind of décor.

To give you a picture of taste among textile and wallpaper industrialists, a little anecdote, just in passing. On the jury of the 1925 Exhibition, there was a textile we refused. The manufacturer sought me out, and, furiously brandishing his sample, almost set to insulting me. But Monsieur, what do you call modern? and he held up before me the design for his sample.

The drawing represented a Chinese scene, pagoda, rock, dwarf trees, and naturally Chinese characters.

RENÉ HERBST ORGANIZING THE HOME

I still did not understand. He then turns back towards me and says: "It's Chinese all right, but modern Chinese." Timidly, I asked him: "But why modern Chinese?" "Don't you see?" No, I told him. "I put a wireless aerial between two of the pagoda roofs."

Bedroom: These rooms do not need to be large in size. They must above all be well ventilated. We ought to sleep with air wafting over our faces. . . . The bed must be simple. It's the linen that counts, not ornaments. A piece of furniture can be adapted to it in which bed linen and clothing will be kept. Do not forget that a cupboard needs to be aired and not kept tight shut. There too, the occupier has to know how to use volumes tastefully. Colored curtains, a contrasting carpet. That hardly resembles a hospital, does it?

Then we pass to the room set aside for cleanliness. Call it, if you will, the "bathroom." If you are short of space, you'll have to install a shower. One washes much more easily in a shower with a sandstone base than in a bathtub. In the same room, you'll have a sink in which to do the laundry, on the ceiling, a special system (they are not expensive) for drying.

To summarize, if the occupant knows how to use color, he can provide himself with an interior that will be a joy for his family.

The day slums are replaced by healthy housing there will be no more discontent. When everyone can rest after a day's work and enjoy a healthy family life, there will be no more need of newspapers because there will be nothing to report.

Goodbye murder, goodbye theft—one cannot burgle a well-lit house, a house in which all the doors are open and everything can be seen. Society would derive considerable benefit from this way of organizing things, because, in the end, what we desire is inner peace.

RENÉ-HERBST,
Lecture at the CPDT, May 4th, 1932

■ Above: Handwritten title by René Herbst to one of his lectures.
Facing page: *Dining room* at the *Formes Utiles* exhibition at the Musée des Arts Décoratifs, 1949.

FOR A HUMANE ARCHITECTURE

POSTWAR RECONSTRUCTION

After World War II, the destruction of hundreds of thousands of homes had made for a dramatic situation and there was a pressing need to engage industrial techniques in the rebuilding. Events had borne out ideas developed by artists of the modern movement prior to the conflict in the course of researches which, far from being limited to aesthetics, had dealt with methods of providing better living conditions for the greatest number derived from a new technological agenda. And yet Modernist practitioners were baffled by the authorities' ignorance of the predicament as exemplified in their neglecting to solicit help from those most qualified to give it: thus, orders never arrived for those involved in research on the plan for the minimum dwelling, nor for that young galaxy of now unemployed talents—who, in consequence, set its sights on emigration.

"More than 20 years ago, at the Grand Palais, [Henri] Sauvage presented a fully equipped prefabricated cell. Francis Jourdain, the apostle, continues his grand, humane efforts. Perret, Le Corbusier and Jeanneret, Mallet-Stevens, Pingusson, Djo-Bourgeois, Charlotte Perriand, Barret . . . what is being done with their creations? . . . are they perhaps not known!"[11]

Horrified by the plight of the victims of the disaster, Herbst was not only combating deplorable conditions in the urban fabric; as he also noted, "rural life is extraordinarily uncomfortable. . . . There are so many devastated villages in France that it would be as well to start worrying about rebuilding them."[12] And, combining action with words as was his habit, he sat on the committee of the Training School for Rural Architects (EFAR). Loyal to his positions, and in agreement with Le Corbusier for whom "town planning begins with the home at its core,"[13] Herbst insisted that the Rebuilding Progam should not be confined to re-erecting edifices; it had to make substantive efforts as to the housing interior too, as a precondition for equilibrium in the family and in society as a whole. "It is a great shame," he declared, "to see the building sector continuing to tackle external construction first, whereas it

■ Pages 202–203: Cover for the book *Formes Utiles* by André Hermant, published by the Salon des Arts Ménagers, 1959; graphic design Pierre Faucheux.
Page 205: Committed to the effort; René Herbst with veterans of the Second Tank Division (2e DB) in 1946.

is more advisable to proceed from interior to exterior."[14] He acknowledged that such projects would be no easy matter, since a great many parameters must be taken into account. "Fine art schools would have to provide courses on social subjects, dealing with physiology and human biology, and students concerned with interiors must be better informed."[15] Herbst also lamented the lack of training of those whose task was to rebuild a France laid waste. As he wrote to Jaujard, head of the government department dealing with the arts and literature,[16] alerting him to shortcomings in the teaching sector: "Over the forty years I have been battling for homes to be equipped with a view to improving life, which is the basis of any rational architecture, I have grown exceedingly worried." As always, he was spending vast amounts of money but the results were unequal to his expectations and this plea too went unheard. He spared no effort, however, giving lectures, and forever repeating his contention that interior architecture, though the poor relation, was primary. Herbst never allowed these woeful circumstances to bring him down and never lost hope in better times to come. He opened a lecture in which he looked back over his many struggles, struggles that had changed little over the years, by saying:

> "The person before you is a partisan who comes to speak about something he has been defending for more than twenty-five years. . . . Excuse his dearth of talent as a public speaker. And if he raises his voice in defense of his raison d'être . . . it is only because he loves his trade."[17]

1. The vice-presidents were André Hermant and Georges-Henri Pingusson. 2. *Manifeste 1949*, drafted by Georges-Henri Pingusson. 3. *Formes Utiles, Objets de Notre Temps* was held under the high patronage of the Minister of Reconstruction, Eugène Claudius-Petit, at the time vice-president of the Union Centrale des Arts Décoratifs. 4. Proposals for the 1937 Exhibition which were not adopted. 5. Francis Jourdain, *Projet pour une Exposition*, 1936. Quoted as an epigraph to the catalog, *Formes Utiles*, MAD, 1949. 6. "To uphold in France the culture of those arts that pursue the realization of the beautiful in the useful" was the goal that the founders of the Union Centrale des Beaux-Arts Appliqués à l'Industrie set themselves, before it became, following its amalgamation with the Société du Musée des Arts Décoratifs, the Union Centrale des Arts Décoratifs in 1882. Among the means implemented: the constitution of a collection of art objects, masterpieces from the Middle Ages to the contemporary period, including a substantial proportion of Islamic pieces, and a library, with the purpose of educating artists and public alike. See Yvonne Brunhammer, *Le Beau dans l'utile* (Paris: Gallimard, 1992). 7. Lecture by André Hermant, typed text, René Herbst Archives. 8. André Hermant, *Formes Utiles* (Paris: Éditions du Salon des arts ménagers, 1959). 9. Hermant, lecture. 10. "Portraits de décorateurs," *Revue de l'Ameublement*. 11. Untitled manuscript, René Herbst Archives. 12. *L'Architecture intérieure*, René Herbst Archives. 13. Le Corbusier, *La Charte d'Athènes*, 1941. 14. *Bâtir la France* (November 7, 1946). 15. Ibid. 16. Letter to M. Jaujard, *directeur* of Les Arts et des Lettres, March 20, 1950, René Herbst Archives. 17. Lecture to *Les Amis de l'Art*, November 19, 1945.

Il y a autant de beautés
qu'il y a de manières habituelles
de chercher le bonheur.

Stendhal.

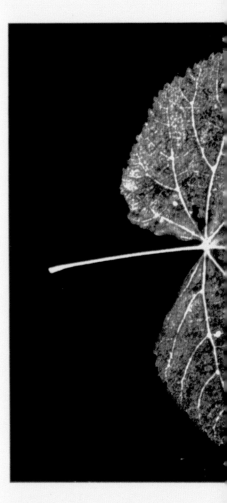

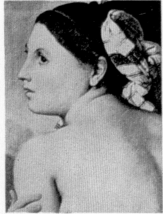

FORMES

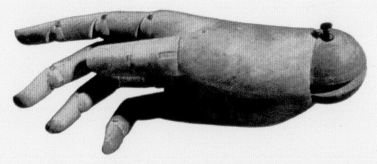

UTILES

INTERIOR ARCHITECTURE AS "SOCIAL ART"

"No obstacle is insurmountable when one wants to offer mankind the well-being it aspires to." RENÉ HERBST[18]

The self-professed aim of the modern movement was to pave the way for the emergence of a "new man" perfectly adapted to his age, and to strive for a modern, classical art that would foment "a new humanism," as attested by the CIAM congress.[19] Faced with growing evidence of the negative repercussions of modern city life—poor air quality, noise, the distance between home and work—Herbst felt that the "cell for living" would become a vital element in human existence. Never wavering from his early ideas, the focus of his endeavors was the equipment of house and home, which in turn implied "composing biologically with the laws [governing] the harmony between body and mind."[20] The elimination of superfluous decoration would leave more room for works of art. The thread running through René Herbst's career is a desire to start from "the inside towards the outside," and so arrive at total architecture. As he often said: "One has to begin with the detail of life." Outraged at the "slums" in which the majority of the French languished, he remained steadfast, protesting that improved living conditions for the population would, by the same token, eliminate social problems.[21] Herbst liked to quote Jean Giraudoux who, in a foreword to the Athens Charter, had written:

"On the pretext of putting civic rights and concerns before urban ones, a terrible inequality has been created—one in human dignity."[22]

René Herbst's life was one of unrelenting combat, devoted body and soul to architecture as a truly social art. "Never forget, I am a partisan . . ."

---

18. *L'Architecture humaine*, manuscript, René Herbst Archives. 19. "[The undersigned architects] have joined forces [so as to] restore architecture to its rightful place, one that is economic and sociological in nature and entirely in the service of the individual." Extract from the first CIAM congress at La Sarraz, 1928. 20. Lecture, René Herbst Archives. 21. He was also interested in studies carried out by hygienists on human physiological needs as regards air, light, and water, and on the effects of noise and radiation. See the report produced by Dr. Winter for the CIAM congress at Bergamo in 1949 that describes the implications of such needs for the construction field. 22. Jean Giraudoux, "Discours liminaire," *La Charte d'Athènes*, 1941.

1891 1928

1891   March 18: birth of René Herbst in Paris
Studies architecture in Paris

1908   Internship at an architect's in London
Participates in the Franco-Britannic exhibition
Internship in Frankfurt, Germany

1913   Mobilized into the air force untill 1919, then reservist

1919   October 20: marries Eugénie Henriette Guigard

1921   November–December. Salon d'Automne: *Coin de repos*. Room with trompe l'oeil bow window and alcove. Natural wood furniture varnished gray with green fillets, dressing table, column supporting a dome light, wallpaper with a pattern matching the covers on folding-screen and seats

1922   November–December. Salon d'Automne: Fitting room with Madeleine Vionnet
February–April. 13th Salon des Artistes Décorateurs: Bureau

1923   Galeries Lafayette: first cut-out store dummies (for men)
May–July. 14th Salon des Artistes Décorateurs,
Urban Art section: Boutique, shop front, and interior for a shoe shop (Perugia), in collaboration with Siégel
"As much skill has been exercised here as in the design of a doorway or a jewel," Yvanohé Rambosson, *Comœdia*. "This store holds the promise of an aesthetics of the street" Léandre Vaillat, *Le Temps*
Furniture section: mahogany and lemon-tree pieces with silver-plated ornaments
November–December. Salon d'Automne,
Urban Art section: two storefronts
Shop for the bootmaker Perugia

1923   Shop for a potter (with Rigault): "The potter's corner, nicely arranged, in reinforced cement and terracotta." Yvanohé Rambosson, *Comœdia*

1924   Awarded the Blumenthal Foundation of America prize for his contribution to the exhibition, *La Pensée française*
May–July. 15th Salon des Artistes Décorateurs: Dining room in varnished mahogany
November–December. Salon d'Automne,
Urban Art section: Public square and ten shops (overseen by Robert Mallet-Stevens). Boutique Siégel; Madeleine Vionnet, dressmaking; Perugia, shoes; Crabette, clothing
Musée Galliera: Silhouette dummies cut out of wood for garment display; designed by Herbst, manufactured by Siégel: "The silhouette dummy is cut out of a plank of wood . . . the hair appears soberly styled around a head that can be moved and be viewed from the front, neck, or in profile. The arms too can be adjusted. A sensational novelty!"

1925   April–October. International Exhibition of the Modern Decorative and Industrial Arts, Paris. Member of admissions jury
Secretary to the Exhibition steering committee
Five luxury boutiques on the Alexander III Bridge: Pleyel (pianos), Siégel (store fitting), Cusenier (liqueurs), Paul Dumas (textiles), René-Herbst (decoration)
Awarded two *diplômes d'honneur*. Gold Medal for architecture, and Silver and Bronze Medals

1926   January. New York, Architectural League, Fine Art Building: *The Modern Dwelling and its Interior Decoration*
Presentation of work by architects Laprade, Proust, Sauvage, and Selmersheim, with the participation of architect-decorators R. Herbst, P. Chareau, A. Groult, G. L. Jaulmes, and J. E. Ruhlmann

Siégel, 1926: scarf by Sonia Delaunay. *Lady's bureau*, Musée des Arts Décoratifs competition, 1928. Window-dressing for Paul Brandt, 1929.

1926 February. Musée Galliera: *Furniture for the Average Frenchman.* Varnished oak gueridon table for mass production. Washable fabric hanging. "In a small-scale exhibition, we wanted to provide an overview of what furniture for 'the average Frenchman' might look like." (Henri Clouzot). Furniture (priced) is shown

    May–July. 16th Salon des Artistes Décorateurs: a gallery with stores for Worth, Lanvin, Jenny, Callot. Dummies André Vigneau, in collaboration with Siégel. Fashion stores fitted out with sawtooth displays

    June. Musée Galliera: *Modern Bronze and Copper.* Shows a ceiling light, wall lamp, and standing floor lamp

    November–December. Salon d'Automne: *Engineer's office.* A study in insulation, using rubber flooring and wall-facing, with a metal sheet and tubing desk, tubular leather chairs," in collaboration with Électro-Câble

    Silk store, with Siégel's. "Patently harks back to the blackface revues . . . A squadron of three vanilla-colored mannequins . . . stand out against three separate screens of cinnamon-colored wood, with a darker inlay of exotic foliage that complete the colonial look," *L'Affiche*, November 1926

    December. Musée Galliera: *Décor for Life*

1927 May–July. 17th Salon des Artistes Décorateurs: Hotel lobby with "ten cannily lit vitrines presenting luxury goods, fan-shaped due to the restricted space, adjacent to a hotel lobby." *Paris-Soir*, June 6, 1927

    November. Salon d'Automne, entrance rotunda: Boutique

    Publishes *Présentation* (Éditions Parade), preface by Henri Clouzot

    President of the Confederation of Modern Artist-Decorators (Chambre Syndicale)

    Awarded a Gold Medal by the French Society for the Encouragement of Art and Industry

    Director of the journal, *Parade, revue du décor de la rue*

1927–32 Private commissions for interiors: Rosenberg, Aga Khan, Peissi, Aghion, Schneider

1928 February–April. Musée des Arts Décoratifs: *The Lady's Desk and Chair* competition followed by an exhibition. 80 projects presented, six awarded prizes and executed, including Herbst's in wood, nickel-plate, and leather

    May–July. 18th Salon des Artistes Décorateurs: Exhibition by the group heralding the UAM

René Herbst: *Smoking-room* comprising nickel-plated steel and varnished wood furniture, with steel velvet-seated chairs

"The association between René Herbst, Djo-Bourgeois, and Mlle Perriand . . . breaks with the outmoded aestheticism of their predecessors. [. . .] they] form part of an avant-garde movement that owes very little to their elders." Waldemar George

"Just as people in 1900 were possessed of a Nature superstition, these have one for machines. [. . .] Djo-Bourgeois, René Herbst, and Charlotte Perriand took as their emblem a bit-brace that they placed in the vestibule." Léandre Vaillat, *Le Temps*, June 1928

    Presentation of a Siégel store dummy carved by André Vigneau

    October. 5th Salon de la Radiophonie, Grand Palais

Herbst sets up a "modern" broadcasting studio; an "attraction much-appreciated by visitors."

    November–December. Salon d'Automne,

    Advertising section: Robj (curios)

Dining-room: nickel-plated steel chairs stretched in Havana brown, walls painted white and yellow, lighting provided by a suspension lamp that drew great attention from critics:

"A device with two wings whose curves have been carefully calculated to reflect the light and that are redolent of the sweeping, contemporary lines of automobiles and airplanes." *Comœdia*, January 15, 1929

"A simple nickel cylinder flanked by reflectors resembling the wings of a soaring gull." *La Liberté*

1929 1934

1929 June. Foundation of the Union des Artistes Modernes (UAM), Assembly held at Hélène Henry's, rue des Grands-Augustins, Paris

Member of the Board

November. Salon de l'Habitation, porte de Versailles: metal furniture

November. Salon d'Automne, *Small living-room* with a suspension lamp. "René Herbst has not been afraid to leave visible the frosted bulb with which his appliance is fitted." Revue *Lux*, December 1929

Shop display for Isabey's (perfumes), faubourg Saint-Honoré: "Big stylized letters in red enclosed in a metal rim forming a pediment above Isabey's frontage attract the bystander's gaze. These windows are both graced with luminous, silvered tables that stand out against the plain background of a folding screen of similar color . . . aluminum . . . furniture as well as for the stair rail, partially hidden from view." Pierre Parceval, *Paris Presse*, December 6, 1929

Shop display for Luminex, Paris

1930–33 Renovation of the Aga Khan's private residence, 55 rue Scheffer in Paris

May. Creation of the Union des Artistes Modernes (UAM), announced in the press following the secession of 25 members of the Société des Artistes Décorateurs

June. Musée des Arts Décoratifs, 1st UAM exhibition: *Salon de Musique*: mahogany and nickel-plated metal piano, bridge table, top covered with green broadcloth, nickel-plated metal chairs with green elastic strapping (sandows), set on a sloping black floor

At the same time, the Salon des Artistes Décorateurs presents the German Werkbund

"The UAM exhibition allows one to compare two methods, one German, the other French—two methods that converge towards the same ideal." Yvanohé Rambosson

November. Liège, International Exhibition, Presentation for French heavy metal industries of cast-iron piping for water conduits and heavy-duty sheet metal for naval construction. "The collaboration between engineer and artist results in works whose austere beauty, today, can no longer be gainsaid. The astonishing impression of uncomplicated order, of precision, of clarity . . . is to the satisfaction of technicians, artists, and the public alike. This last understands that steel, in which rails, bridges, ships, engines, cars, armatures, and rolling stock, such as locomotives and coaches, are made, is necessary to sustain everyday life." (Herbst) "We are living in the century of steel," *Nord Industriel*, November 1, 1930

1931 February. *Store display and Window dressing*, lecture at the regional school of architecture and industrial art, Grenoble

Fits out the Section Métropolitaine: metallurgy, steel industries, with OTUA

May. 2nd UAM exhibition, Galerie Georges Petit Dining room in rosewood and chromium-plated metal, Aga Khan model "This time, our modern architects and interior decorators show us locomotives, airplanes, dynamos and Chicago's silos, saying: 'These are our masters and our models. These are our Parthenons, our cathedrals.'" François Fosca, *Je suis partout*, May 20, 1931

October. Colonial Exhibition, Paris

November–December. Salon d'Automne: *Dining room and corner of a hall* "René Herbst presents this relatively modestly priced dining room, not in the way of a reconstitution, but as a storefront on inclined planes and under shop-window lighting; yet over such parsimony he festoons vivacious notes of green leather, and fabrics by Mme. Hélène Henry." Léandre Vaillat, *Le Temps*, November 27, 1931

"Herbst's 'roll-on, roll-off' display is inevitably destined to bamboozle the masses, though the furniture itself has been calculated with rigorous logic." *Beaux-Arts*, November 25, 1931

UAM logo by Pierre Legrain, 1929. Nest of tables in a private house, 1933. 3rd Salon de la Lumière, 1935, invitation by Francis Bernard.

1932 Preparations for the 1937 Exhibition of Art and Technology. Secretary for the study committee and member of the jury for the concept competition

March. Musée des Arts Décoratifs, 3rd UAM exhibition: *Dressing-table* for the Princess Aga Khan

"The 'theoretical intoxication' that grips both the Werkbund and *L'Esprit Nouveau* . . . is it a passing fad or a style? These dentist, these sanatorium chairs, this Puritanism, the architectonic bareness of this 'machine for living,' is it the effort of beginners, of idlers—or a truly new mode of living," Louis Vauxcelles, *L'Excelsior*, February 1932

Dressing table "in which the mirror encased in a metal armature far more closely resembles the fearsome door to a safe deposit box than an acolyte for female coquetry." Georges Belt, *Oran Matin*
"Chairs with backs made of elastic straps for athletes." Charles Kunstler, *Ric et Rac*
"The dictatorship of the architect-engineer is definitive." *Le Crapouillot*
June. Musée Galliera: *Metals in Art*
Bureau-bookcase in mahogany and nickel, model for the Aga Khan

"The problem facing contemporary decorative art is precisely this: is it a laboratory creation or does it possess the characteristics of a style? Divided by personal rivalries, opposed in both principles and doctrines, modern interior decorators nevertheless fall into two distinct categories, the ones upholsterers, the others architects. The first concocts combinations of luxury accessories; the second orders forms and lines. The former clothes—the latter clears out." Guillaume Janneau, *L'Exportateur français*, October 13, 1932

December. Rabat, Morocco: *French Decorative Art*

1933 January–February. 1st Exposition de l'Habitation, Grand Palais, Organized by the Salon des Arts Ménagers and the journal, *L'Architecture d'Aujourd'hui*

1933 June. Galerie Art et Décoration: *Metal Furniture*
Henri Clouzot considers Herbst as the "leader of the school."
"To study René Herbst is to recount the history of the avant-garde decorative arts over the last ten years. As to the use of metal in furniture . . . in 1926 he was the first by his example to demonstrate its legitimacy. But far from deriving inspiration from interior decorators on the other side of the Rhine, as has been alleged, his chairs, solidly set on four load points, have no more links with German cantilever chairs than the rounded corners, and harmonious curves of his tables and daybeds have with the angular or aggressive forms of similar pieces made abroad." *L'Industriel savoisien*, April 1, 1933

June–July. 4th UAM Exhibition, Galerie de la Renaissance
Presentation of the Furniture section
Photographs of the Aga Khan's private residence, rue Scheffer, Paris

November–December. Salon d'Automne: gaming table with chairs; Photographs of the Aga Khan's private residence

1934 February–March. *French Decorative Art*, Galerie Bernheim-Jeune. *Bahut-vaisselier* ("Welsh dresser" or sideboard) from the vestibule of the Aga Khan's residence, mahogany with metal handles

July 14: *Pour l'art moderne*, launch of the manifesto of the Union des Artistes Modernes

"In addition to the old duet of wood and stone, which we have never neglected, we have also attempted to assemble a quartet featuring cement, glass, metal, and electricity, a harmonious quartet whose principles we have sought to determine and whose chords we have attempted to work out." UAM *Manifesto*

October. 2nd Salon de la Lumière
Office Central Electrique (OCEL), boulevard Haussmann: A luminous water fountain in the exhibition hall whose jets intermingle with beams of light

1934 1945

1934   November–February. 12th Salon des Arts Ménagers–2nd Exposition de l'Habitation, Grand Palais
In conjunction with the antique-dealers exhibition, a group show by architects and interior decorators, in an effort to reconcile art and daily life
Presents metal furniture in the Galerie des Décorateurs

"Shall we raise the household arts to the level of the fine arts or shall we consider the fine arts as the first among household arts? . . .The salon derives great benefit from this salutary duality." *Beaux-Arts,* February 1, 1935

November. Salon d'Automne: steel boat cabins
René Herbst presents a 1st class cabin

"The steel-walled cabin with steel furniture corresponds . . . to a necessity and not at all to a desire for ornamental fantasy. As for the decorative effect, it is obtained by harmonious relationships between volume and line, by the contrast between polished metal and matt paint." Maximilien Gauthier, *Les Nouvelles Littéraires*

1935   January 15: Inauguration of the Musée de l'Hygiène, passive defense section. Appointed technical curator
March 1st. Salon de l'Enseigne: Project for the silversmith Raymond Templier. The Retrospective and Modern Exhibition
April–November. Universal and International Exhibition, Brussels. In the Metropolitan France Pavilion, the fine arts join decorative art under the responsibility of André Fréchet. Maurice Dufrène heads the "modern decoration" section with as its theme the French family home and a prototype middle-class apartment. The model dwelling is composed of a vestibule, a hall, two galleries, a drawing-room, a dining-room, office, several bedrooms and a bathroom
Group presentation for a young man's apartment. René Herbst: Fitness zone, stainless-steel washable furniture and accessories, white

linoleum flooring, Fernand Léger painting on the wall. French metallurgy and electricity group with OTUA: 3,937 ft.^{2} (1,200 m^2)

"René Herbst has been called revolutionary. . . He is certainly the man who knows how to use all the resources of steel in decorative art, who has best sensed the beauty of plain metal, and the nuances of its reflections. . . . A colossal, intelligently arranged sheaf of metallurgical components in their raw state, sheets, beams, etc., that flaunt the sheer beauty of the untreated material. A large photographic panel presents every metal product, from a frame for the steamer *Normandie* and a carcass for a building, to Raymond Templier's steel jewelry. And all this is in color: white, steel, ultramarine underscored in vermilion. In the electricity section, René Herbst presents lighting [and] wireless, in a colorful white, beige, and red decor." Renée Moutard-Uldry, *Beaux-Arts*, April 26, 1935

Elected Chevalier of the Légion d'honneur (Beaux-Arts section)
President of the Confederation of Artist-Decorators
October. 3rd Salon de la Lumière. UAM exhibits under the direction of Robert Mallet-Stevens and André Salomon
René Herbst: Colored glass panel in the shape of an arc of a circle with tubing and flower-stand [reproduced in *Art et Décoration,* p. 414]

"Light has now earned the right to a place of its own in contemporary decoration, rendering life in interiors more intense and creating on avenues and boulevards a nocturnal décor through multicolored signs with luminescent tubes." André Bloc, *Journal de l'Ameublement,* November 1935

December 10. "Sur un manifeste," article in *La Revue Mondiale*
"A plea for an art movement and a style that have recently been shown to be bankrupt. The discourse [by Louis Chéronnet] is thus a funeral oration. . . . Modern art is one hundred percent sick." Waldemar George

International Exhibition, Brussels, 1935, collage by Herbst. Industrial French metallurgy, Liège 1930. Children's school furniture, 1949.

1935   Boulogne-sur-Seine town hall, refit for the registry office (weddings)

1936   Store display: Jean Puiforcat, goldsmith, Paris
Member of the State purchases commission
Member of the jury for the Ecole des Beaux-Arts, Lille
November. Salon d'Automne: school furniture exhibition by the UAM Direction René Herbst, with the collaboration of the OTUA
May. Musée Galliera: *Invitation au voyage*. New displays of steamer cabins

1937   February. 4th Exposition de l'Habitation:
"The UAM and school furniture"; Herbst returns to the theme of school furniture with a broader remit than at the 1936 Salon d'Automne

May–November. International Exhibition of Arts and Technology, Paris
Member of the admissions and awards jury
Architect for Group I Class II, for libraries and literary events at the Trocadéro. Oversees an exhibition space of 6.2 square miles (10 km²): Advertising pavilion, interior exhibition fixtures
Centre des métiers d'art: stand for Maubeuge (iron company); Paul Martial (publishers) and Puiforcat, Jean Luce, and Charles Moreau (stores). OTUA: UAM Pavilion: head of planning and interior fixtures. Exhibits his *Studio furniture*. A multipurpose piece of furniture in mahogany and sycamore [purchased in 1938 by the Mobilier National, in deposit with the Musée des Arts Décoratifs]: open, it offers a drop-flap for writing, with space for telephone, bookshelf, suspension files, radio, and phonograph; closed, it looks like a pier table with a smooth, sober front, studded with metal mounts constituting the handles that appear to support the piece when shut, on which a sculpture or other object may be placed

"Industrial mass production, this is our hope. For too long, art and industry have stood apart. For too long, it has been accepted that what is beautiful has to be extortionate and that what is cheap has to be ugly." G. Brunon-Guardia, *La Liberté*, October 9, 1937

10th anniversary of the review, *Parade*

1938   November–December. Salon d'Automne: *Studio furniture*; School furniture. Participation in the Prefabrication section
This Salon d'Automne "is a well-behaved little show, slightly behind the times, whereas in 1900, the same Salon seemed innovative." M. B., *Toute l'édition*, November 19, 1938

1939   New York, International Exhibition: French literature, graphic arts, and steel industries sections. Exhibition architect-designer

1940   Volunteer in the air force: demobilized July 28, 1940

1942   Salon des Artistes Décorateurs: establishes the graphic arts section
Vice-president of the Société des Artistes Décorateurs
Founding member of the Front National des Artistes Décorateurs Créateurs (FNADC) opposed to all collaboration with the occupying forces

1943   Fits out the reading-room at the Maison de la Chimie, Paris

1944   November. Salon d'Automne: *Architecture 44*
December 1944–February 1945 Musée des Arts Décoratifs: *Artists of the Book and Printing*

1945   Barcelona trade fair: in charge of the Book section
Mass-produced furniture, lecture in Switzerland

1945 1982

1945 Member of the board of the Union des Intellectuels

1946 Produces the exhibitions:
Hitler's Crimes, Paris (Grand Palais) and London
The Resistance, Hôtel Berlitz, Paris
The 2nd Tank Division, Paris
November. Salon d'Automne: graphic arts, architecture and equipment sections

1946–48 Private installations: Bloch, Gessler, Poncet, Monyal

1946–58 President of the UAM
Bezon Chapel: interior
Foundation of the "Club Mallet-Stevens," 12, rue Mallet-Stevens, Paris 16th

1947 Member of the committee of the École de Formation des Architectes Ruraux (EFAR)

1948 February–March. Musée des Arts Décoratifs: *Iron and Steel in Housing*
November. Salon d'Automne: Tables and chairs
Delagrave residence, rue Scheffer, Paris: remodeling

1949 UAM *Manifesto* published by the "Club Mallet-Stevens"
April–May. Musée des Arts Décoratifs: *Sarre, Center of Arts and Crafts*
November. Salon d'Automne: Classroom
December 1949–February 1950. Musée des Arts Décoratifs: *Formes Utiles*
Shop and restaurant display (inc. Prunier, Paris)

1950–66 President of *Formes Utiles*

1950 February–March. Salon des Arts Ménagers: kitchenette-dining room in molded plywood

1951 Constructs a housing project in Brest

1952 The Sorbonne, Paris: exhibition dedicated to the UAM mounted to tour the United States

1953 Rome, French national agricultural show: chief exhibition architect
Fits out the Restaurant Prunier, rue Duphot, Paris

1954 10th Milan Triennial: Vice-president of the international jury. Architect for the French entries
Steel industries exhibition, Paris
February–March. Salon des Arts Ménagers: prefabricated house on a metal frame over 223 ft.² (68 m²) on the Esplanade at the Invalides

1955 March–May. Musée des Arts Décoratifs: *Art and advertising worldwide,* exhibition designer; organized by the Alliance graphique internationale (AGI)
Helsinborg, Sweden, French exhibition of applied arts: Vice-president
February–March. Salon des Arts Ménagers: realizes the "Bâtiment du Bois" (timber display)
Fits out the Restaurant Prunier, London

1956 Publishes: *25 années UAM: 1930–1955,* Éditions du Salon des Arts Ménagers
Glassmaking and *Formes Utiles,* lecture under the auspices of the 4th International Glass Congress, Paris
October 1956–January 1957, 1st Triennial of French Contemporary Art: Art and Technology—*Formes Utiles*

Milan Triennial, 1954. *Le Bois,* Salon des Arts Ménagers, 1955, collage by René Herbst. OTUA Pavilion, Moscow, 1961.

1957   11th Milan Triennial: Architect for the French entries
Vice-president of the jury
            Salon des Arts Ménagers: builds warehouses at Nanterre

1957–64 Member of the steering committee of the Union Centrale des Arts Décoratifs

1958   April–October. Brussels, International and Universal Exhibition Architect responsible for the sections: French thought; French steel industries; Science
            Johannesburg, international exhibition: French steel industry with the OTUA
            Resigns from the UAM, which is "put on hold"

1959   Salon de l'Emballage (packaging)

1960   12th Milan Triennial: Architect for the French entries

1961   Moscow, International Exhibition: constructs the French steel industries pavilion together with the OTUA

1962   June. Musée des Arts Décoratifs, *Everyday Life*

1963   Ghent: *Forms and Industry,* superintendent for the French contingent
            June–October. Musée des Arts Décoratifs, *Formes industrielles,* international selection
            Besançon, Exhibition 1925: commissioner
            Salon des Arts Ménagers: constructs a second industrial building, in Nanterre

1964   13th Milan Triennial: member of the planning committee
            Warsaw: Forms, Industries, Urbanism, Architecture,

Decoration, superintendent for the French contribution
            London, International Exhibition of the Graphic Arts

1965   Member of the committee of the SEAI, on juries for various sections

1966   14th Milan Triennial: French delegate on the preparation committee
            Genoa, *Eurodomus,* pilot exhibition for the modern house: French delegate

1972   Death of his wife

1982   August: his archives donated to Union Centrale des Arts Décoratifs
            September 29: death of René Herbst in Paris.

RENÉ HERBST THE ARCHIVES

Shortly before his death in 1982, René Herbst donated his archives, partly to the Bibliothèque des Arts Décoratifs, and partly to the Bibliothèque Forney, the remainder, together with the furniture from his studio on rue Chateaubriand, being put up for sale at the Galerie Maria de Beyrie. In addition, the gift made to the Union Centrale des Arts Décoratifs for the Library included the complete archives of the Union des Artistes Modernes (UAM) of which René Herbst had been a founder member and then president. The René Herbst Archives at the Bibliothèque des Arts Décoratifs provide great insight into a career lasting forty years that began in 1921 at the Salon d'Automne, continuing to his last large-scale project, the French Pavilion at the 1961 International Exhibition in Moscow.

These photographs, press cuttings, letters, graphic documents, albums, sketch books, and photomontages of works made by Herbst himself, as well as texts (manuscript versions of publications and lectures), offer a wealth of documentation. Of particular interest are the nine folders and twenty-three boxes of photographs arranged by category—featuring exhibitions, furniture, interiors, stores—and the sixteen scrapbooks of press cuttings classified and glued by René Herbst himself covering the period 1921–1939 on a series of catalogs of the first UAM exposition in 1930. These large-size albums measuring 1 ft. x 9.6 in. (32 x 24.5 cm) allow one to relive, practically day to day, the growth of the modern movement, the lively debates and the observations and questions of contemporaries concerning the radical changes in everyday life as a consequence of the increased mechanization of the urban environment.

Their consultation has provided the thread that runs through this account of René Herbst's career, and, by the same token, of the emergence of a new way of living in the contemporary world, which the present publication seeks to address.

These holdings, referenced under the inventory number 8832, complement publications by René Herbst and numerous journals on the decorative arts containing articles about him that are already to be found in the collections of the Bibliothèque des Arts Décoratifs.

Inventory of the Fonds René Herbst

A. Photographs	1. Box, 8832 A1-A23
	2. Folders, 8832 A24-A32
B. Notebooks	1. Hotel Carlton, 1933, 8832 B1
	2. Pleyel Pianos, 8832 B2
	3. Brussels [International Exhibition 1935], 8832 B3
	4. French Graphic Art, New York [International Exhibition 1939], 8832 B4
	5. Art teaching in Sarre [1946–1949], 8832 B5
	6. Prefabricated house, Salon des Arts Ménagers [1954], 8832 B6
	7. Wood, Salon des Arts Ménagers [1955], 8832 B7
	8. Moscow [International Exhibition 1961], 8832 B8
	9. Metal and wood furniture, 8832 B9
	10. Steel chairs, 8832 B10
	11. A 40-year career/40 photographs, 8832 B11
C. Press	Albums 8832 C1-C16
	Boxes 8832 C17-C18
D. Writings	Box 8832 D1
E. Personal documents	Boxes 8832 E1-E2
F. UAM Archives	8832 F1-F10
	. Statutes, register of minutes of the General Assemblies 1929-1953; folders containing minutes 1954-1956, 8832 F1
	. General Assemblies 8832 F2
	. Admissions requests 8832 F3
	. Club Mallet-Stevens; Jeunes de l'UAM 8832 F4
	. Exhibitions 1930-1953 France; USA project 1952 8832 F5
	. Accounts 8832 F6
	. Individual dossiers 8832 F7
	. Correspondence, preparatory texts, notes, press cuttings: CSADM/SPAD, *Formes Utiles*/SAD, 1941; Congress of Industrial Esthetics 1953; Centre de Documentation de l'Habitation, 1952 88832 F8
	. Brochures, graphic documents 8832 F9
	. Press 8832 F10

Published books by René Herbst [Bibliothèque des Arts Décoratifs shelf marks]
. *Devantures, vitrines, installations de magasins à l'Exposition de 1925*. Paris: Charles Moreau, n. d.   Y 751
. *Présentation: Le décor de la rue*, vol.1. Paris: Parade, 1927.   UU 109
. *Présentation: Le décor de la rue*, vol. 2, publ. Parade, 1929.   UU 109
. *Nouvelles devantures et agencements de magasins parisiens*, 5 vols. Paris: Charles Moreau, 1933.   UU 254
. *Devantures et installations de magasins*, Paris: Charles Moreau, n. d.   UU 253
. *Boutiques et magasins*, collection "L'art international d'aujourd'hui", n° 8. Paris: Charles Moreau, n. d.   RA 45
. *Jean Puiforcat*, Paris: Flammarion, 1951.   Y 1335
. *Pierre Chareau*, Paris: Salon des Arts Ménagers, 1954.   XN 381
. *25 années UAM*, Paris: Salon des Arts Ménagers, 1956.   XW 15

Revues of decorative arts — Main titles 1880–1960 [Bibliothèque des Arts Décoratifs shelf marks]
. *Revue des arts décoratifs*, in 1902 absorbed into *L'Art décoratif*   D 34 – Q 642
. *Art et Décoration*   JP 9
. *Art et Industrie*   T 976
. *Art et Industrie. Revue générale des industries de luxe et des arts appliqués à la maison*   JP 186
. *L'Architecture d'Aujourd'hui*   JP 75
. *L'art aujourd'hui* (1949); became *Aujourd'hui* (1955–1967)   JP 203
. *L'art décoratif moderne. Revue des arts appliqués à l'industrie*   T 752
. *L'art décoratif pour tous*   TT 238
. *Le décor d'aujourd'hui*   JP 23
. *Les échos d'industries d'art*   JP 98
. *L'Esprit Nouveau*   XA 29
. *Lux. La revue de l'éclairage*   Y 873
. *Meubles et décors. Journal de l'ameublement*   JP 208
. *Mobilier et décoration*   JP 173
. *Parade*   JP 259

Selected bibliography [Bibliothèque des Arts Décoratifs shelf marks]
. Moussinac, Léon. *Intérieur III*. Paris: A. Lévy, 1925.   T 891
. Moreau, Charles. *Union des Artistes Modernes*, 1929.   BR 11621
. *Union des Artistes Modernes*. Exhibition catalog. Musée des Arts Décoratifs, 1930.   BR 9428
. *Formes Utiles*. Exhibition catalog. Musée des Arts Décoratifs, 1949.   BR 14606
. *Formes Utiles*. Salon des Arts Ménagers catalogs, 1951–1980.   Y 1457
. *Art et Publicité dans le monde*. Exhibition organized by the International Graphic Alliance,
Musée des Arts Décoratifs, 1955.   BR 15346
. *Triennale d'art français contemporain. Art et Techniques: Formes Utiles*. Exhibition catalog,
Musée des Arts Décoratifs, 1956.   BR 15763
. Le Corbusier. *La Charte d'Athènes*. Paris: Minuit, 1957.   XS 116/4
. Hermant, André. *Formes Utiles*. Paris: Éditions du Salon des Arts Ménagers, 1959.   XQ 69
. Renous, Pascal. *Portraits de décorateurs*. Revue de l'Ameublement, 1965.   XW 273
. *Formes industrielles*. Exhibition catalog, Musée des Arts Décoratifs, 1963.   XS 153
. *Charlotte Perriand, un art de vivre*. Musée des Arts Décoratifs/Flammarion, 1985.   XT 1485
. Barré-Despond, Arlette. *UAM*. Paris: Le Regard, 1986.   XV 457/11
. Barré-Despond, Arlette and Suzanne Tise. *Jourdain*. Paris: Le Regard, 1988.   XV 457/15
. *Les Années UAM 1929–1958*. Exhibition catalog, Musée des Arts Décoratifs, 1988.   XU 2088
. Goguel, Solange. *René Herbst*. Paris: Le Regard, 1990.   XV 457/16
. Graffin, Laurence. *André Mare. Carnets de guerre, 1914-1918*. Paris: Herscher, 1996.   MC 1522
. Brunhammer, Yvonne. *Le Beau dans l'utile: un musée des arts décoratifs*. Paris: Gallimard, 1992.   XR 703/24
. Rubini, Constance. "'Parade,' la revue de décor de la rue," in *Design et étalage*. Paris: VIA/Seuil, 2002.   MC 9023/9
. Schlansker Kolosek, Lisa. *L'Invention du chic. Thérèse Bonney et le Paris Moderne*. Paris: Norma, 2002.   MC 2268

Photographic credits

Whenever they are known, the photographers of the images belonging to the René Herbst archives in the Bibliothèque des Arts Décoratifs reproduced in this book are listed below:

Page 5: Photo Paul Martial
Page 15: 18, 19, 20: Photos Rep
Page 27: Photo Wulffing
Page 41: Photo Illustration Paris
Page 52–53: Photo Rep
Page 55: Photo Illustration Paris
Pages 59, 60–61: Photos Lucien Aubert
Page 62–63: Photo Jean Collas
Page 76–77: Photo Lacheroy
Pages 80, 81, 83, 85, 91: Photos Jean Collas
Page 92-93: Photo Rep
Page 98-99: Photo Jean Collas
Page 100: Photo Tabard
Page 105: Photo Rep
Pages 109, 110, 111, 112-113, 114, 115, 116–117, 118, 119, 122, 123, 141,
142, 143, 144, 145, 146, 168–169, 170–171: Photos Jean Collas
Page 178-179: Photo Lacheroy
Page 183: Photo Kollar
Page 203: Photo Jean Collas
Page 207 (left): Photo Thérèse Bonney
Page 211 (right): Photo Jean Collas